by Stacey Kole
foreword by Vonette Bright

SHANNON
PUBLISHERS

Seeing Yourself Through God's Eyes
©2001 by Stacey Kole

Published by Shannon Publishers
PO Box 575
Artesia, CA 90702

ShannPubl@aol.com

Printed in the United States of America

International Standard Book Number 0-9638575-4-1

To my mother, Kathy Kole—
This book is her trophy.
(Proverbs 22:6)

God does not view things the way we do. People look at the outward appearance, but the Lord looks at the heart.
1 Samuel 16:7

Contents

Foreword

Stacey Kole is a young woman who has lived a "charmed life" of popularity, beauty, and outstanding ability. I have known her from the time that she was six years of age and have watched her grow and develop into a strikingly beautiful, capable, spiritually sensitive woman. Her accomplishments and honors are many, including reigning as Miss Arizona, and finishing in the top six in the 1998 Miss USA pageant. Many would look at her achievements and assume that she had what it takes to make anyone happy.

Little did I realize the difficulties she was facing in her teenage years. In the pages to follow, Stacey graciously opens the door to her life and discloses some of the deceptive and even dangerous lies she was led to believe. Many in our American culture have come to believe these lies about who we are, our value and our purpose in life. Stacey admitted to her insecurities, sought help and achieved victory over her circumstances. In doing so, God has given her a platform of ministry to help others who are trapped in believing the same lies and who are carrying insecurities and doubts in the secret corners of their hearts.

Stacey takes us back in time through her adolescent years and unveils what she believed about herself and what she relied on for her security and worth. Unfortunately the false perception of self clouds the truth behind God's unique purpose and design for each of our lives.

Stacey's road to victory began when she started to internalize the truth from God's Word about her Creator God and what His purpose was for her life. She chose not to hide her insecurities and worries behind a false image, or fall into the trap of trying to dull her pain with addictive and destructive behaviors. Instead, Stacey put her trust in God and is in the process of allowing the Holy Spirit to transform her heart and mind, molding her into the person God created her to be.

It is great that she opened her life to others who could help and encourage her. Far too often most people keep their concerns to themselves and do not seek or receive help. My teenage granddaughter, Rebecca, having read this book, appreciates her openness and understanding of the problem Stacey faced and the Biblical perspective in which this book is presented. She believes Stacey's testimony will not only help the person who is experiencing similar problems, but that it will help family and friends understand their loved one's problems and provide answers.

The life road Stacey has chosen is available to every one of us as well. May Stacey's assurance of God's purpose for her life be formed in your heart. I believe this book will help do just that.

Vonette Bright
Campus Crusade for Christ / Women Today Radio

Introduction

After winning the 1998 title of Miss Arizona and placing 6th in the national Miss USA competition, my full-time job became traveling across the country as a speaker to university women. The subject I am most commonly asked to address is the importance of a healthy self-image. Some critics think I am the last person in the world who should be talking about something like this, because of my beauty pageant background. They often pose the question, "Why should any woman listen to you? Of course a pageant winner can talk about positive self-image. But what about normal women who don't look like beauty queens? What hope is there for them?

It is a good question, but the reasoning is faulty. Allow me a purely hypothetical story. Imagine a beautiful woman on the cover of Glamour Magazine. She's got a great body with legs that seem to go on forever, gorgeous skin, and thick, curly auburn hair. Now think of your next door neighbor. She's rather overweight, her skin is showing signs of aging, and she can't seem to get rid of that eighties perm. Finally, let's pretend we can read minds. First, we eavesdrop on the thoughts of the neighbor and hear her berate herself for being fat and ugly. Now onto the model's thoughts. We hear her obsessing over the size of her thighs and bottom, convinced that they will cost her her career. She then curses herself for eating too much junk food, vowing she won't eat even a bite until she loses five pounds. When we leave her, she's sitting on the bathroom floor with her face in her hands, sobbing. She mumbles, "I'll never be good enough . . . I never have, never will."

Sounds far-fetched? Is it possible for a gorgeous woman to experience deep stabs of insecurity and low self-worth in the same way that an "average" woman does? I know case after case where the scenario above would be right on the money. Take me for instance . . . .

My resume from childhood to adolescence, in a nutshell, included winning my first beauty pageant at age 11, being Valedictorian of my junior high school, finishing in the Top 10 at the America's Miss T.E.E.N. Pageant, being voted "Most Likely to Succeed" in high school, and performing all over the state of Arizona as a singer and dancer. That's what people saw on paper.

The dark side of my youth was an overwhelming desire for perfection. There was no one who drove me to it; I drove myself. It was as though my worth as a person depended on the number of A's I got and the number of trophies I acquired. So if I wasn't succeeding—whether physically, mentally, or socially—I wasn't happy. In fact, I was down right depressed. But who would have known? No one had the power to read my mind and hear my painful thoughts.

Years later, after seeking counseling for an eating disorder brought on by my ruthless perfectionism, I was able to slowly make the connection that what's on the outside isn't what defines me The beauty inside me does. And that is why people who look like super-models can hate themselves and people whose weight fluctuates as much as Oprah's does can love them-selves.

So in answer to my critics, I ask them one question of my own: "Who is better qualified to talk about self-image than one who on the outside had it all together, but for years was far from that ideal on the inside?" After all, if even the most "perfect" people in the world struggle with feelings of low self worth, then no one is alone. Fat, skinny, short, tall, blonde, brunette, or red-head . . . we all have one thing in common. We need internal beauty to experience true peace and happi-ness. And there's only one way to get that. We must see ourselves through God's eyes. That's why I wrote this book. I want you to make the discovery it took too long for me to make. It was a process for me, and it will likely be a process for you. But that's okay . . . we'll make the journey together.

Stacey Kole

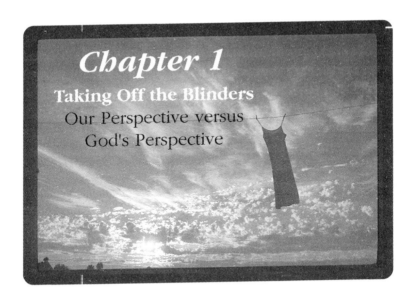

Chapter 1

Taking Off the Blinders
Our Perspective versus God's Perspective

In February of 1998, I flew to Louisiana to compete in the nationally-televised Miss USA Pageant. When I stepped off the plane, I was immediately whisked into a room with fifty other women who were all there for the exact same reason that I was—to win the crown. Looking around the room I saw perfect bodies decked out in DKNY and St. John suits, bouncy, shiny heads of hair that came straight out of a Pantene commercial, and gorgeous faces which would have made Estee Lauder jealous.

"Have you ever been in a national pageant?" whispered the contestant standing next to me.

"I competed in a national teen pageant, but it wasn't televised," I whispered back.

"So you've never really done something like this?" I shook my head no, and she looked relieved. She heard the answer she wanted.

"How about you?" I asked.

"Never."

That was the first and only conversation I had that day that felt remotely real. The rest of the time, I listened to each young woman recite her resume as I smiled and nodded. It was all I could do not to counter with my own. By the time I had talked to about half of the girls, I was no longer surprised to learn that many were professional runway models as well as law or pre-med students. With every new revelation, my heart sank. That night I went to bed feeling completely out of my league. They were smart and beautiful. Maybe I didn't belong there.

Two weeks later I sat with these same women in a similar room. They were still pretty, but the clothes were far more casual, the hair was in ponytails, and the make-up had lightened significantly. This time we weren't swapping resumes; we were sharing fears.

"I felt so intimidated when I first saw y'all," a Miss from the south drawled.

"Me too," chimed a northern contestant. "Everyone looked so beautiful and had accomplished way more than me. I wanted to go home."

Every voice in the room echoed the same sentiment. We had all been scared of each other. We had talked big, but deep inside we had never felt so insecure.

As I listened to the truth spilling forth, I couldn't help but wonder why even the most "perfect" people by society's standards thought so little of themselves. How tragic it seemed that they could only see themselves through the critical eyes of the culture, which never ceased to say that their best was never good enough. Even more disturbing to me that afternoon in Louisiana was realizing that I shared their negative feelings. I too thought I had something to prove to everyone, and I wanted nothing more than to find that approval in their eyes. Sadly, for most of my time at the Miss USA Pageant, I was looking for my identity through distorted lenses.

The Miss USA Pageant of 1998 wasn't the first time I had experienced painful feelings of inadequacy. In fact, I've struggled with the need to prove myself ever since I can remember. But there was one period in my life when my thoughts about myself reached an all time low—and stayed there.

As an active junior in high school, everything about me looked great. I earned straight A's, was voted student council secretary, and to top it off, I was representing my state in my first national pageant—America's Miss T.E.E.N. Life was filled with fun things such as planning dances, singing solos at school assemblies, and taking dance and acting lessons. Because my dad worked as a professional magician, even my job was interesting. I climbed in and out of boxes, was sawed in half, and levitated high above the stage. Any spare time I found would be used up quickly as a community volunteer. I worked in nursing homes, taught children to read, and wrote Bible school curriculum. In fact, when the teen pageant in which I was competing had me total the time I spent doing volunteer work, it totaled over 700 hours in one year. Others referred to me as "the perfect daughter," "the model student," and "the girl who did it all."

I have to admit, I liked all of the attention. It was fun to be thought of as perfect. With each new accomplishment, I felt my self-esteem soar. Since my plates all seemed to be spinning perfectly, I started looking for something new to perfect.

I couldn't help but notice that one area in my life didn't seem up to par. I wasn't generally regarded as the prettiest girl in school. I didn't even have a boyfriend. Sure I was able to get past the pageant judges with my looks. I figured that was probably because there wasn't a swimsuit competition in this particular contest. However, I was certain that if there were, I wouldn't get very far. Consequently I determined that my new goal would be to become the thinnest girl in school. After all, I wasn't really fat to begin with, but there was always room for improvement. I knew one girl in my class was ninety-eight pounds, and that seemed like a reasonable number to beat. Besides, eating in front of people was embarrassing and not very feminine. With my new goal in mind I started drinking diet shakes for breakfast and eating only an apple for lunch.

Before long I was the best in yet another area, because I had more will-power than anyone else. When my friends would eat french fries and candy bars, I looked cool and self-controlled when I refused the junk food. Life was good again . . . or so I thought.

The holidays were ending, as were two hectic months in my young teen life. I returned from the national pageant where I was chosen as a finalist, but not the winner. I headed straight into a week's worth of make-up work and then into final exams. With everything finally finished, I flopped into bed, only to wake up the next morning in an unexplainable fit of tears. When my mom found me, I was crying and shaking uncontrollably. I couldn't speak, or even get out of bed to get ready for school. Finally I whispered three words: "I'm so scared." I kept saying the phrase over and over. Actually, that was an understatement, but it was all I could utter to describe the sheer terror I felt at getting up and going through another day of trying to be perfect and attempting to please everyone around me.

Needless to say, I didn't go to school that day. Instead I ended up in the office of a counselor. My face still streaming with tears, I tried to answer his questions as best as I could.

"No, I never get B's."

"Yes, I'd be devastated if I did."

"Yes, I watch what I eat."

"No, I don't think I have anything like anorexia."

His questions continued for what seemed like hours. He didn't try to hide his diagnosis.

"An extreme perfectionist," he called me.

"Bordering on an eating disorder."

I was just 16, but I had pretty much hit bottom. Doing everything, doing it perfectly, and ultimately trying to physically embody perfection, had turned me a full 180 degrees away from where I wanted to be. Even though my problems had been brewing under the surface for a long time, it seemed that it took only one day for my story book life to turn into a nightmare. I became depressed, restless, fearful, and completely void of confidence. My once very directed life seemed aimless; my personal identity vanished.

It is said that things sometimes have to look down before they can look up. That is the last thing I wanted to hear when my world was crashing in around me. As much as I hated hearing that old cliche, I knew it held much truth. Nearly a decade later, I continue to run into the same old struggles and feelings that I experienced then. They are still painful. The difference, however, is that now I have an entirely new perspective. That fresh perspective didn't come overnight, nor did it come easily. In spite of the pain and struggle, I am truly grateful that I was forced to learn some very valuable, though admittedly painful, lessons.

The number one thing I discovered as a teenager was the same thing I found myself learning all over again at the Miss USA Pageant—we only get heartache and disappointment when we try to find our worth in someone else's eyes. Why do we look to everyone around us for an endorsement of who we are? I'm sure if I took a survey across America, I'd discover that homemakers, business women, college students, mothers, doctors, and lawyers all seek approval in the eyes of others. Is there something programmed into the human mind that makes us compare ourselves to everyone else, only to conclude that we have no hope of measuring up to our unrealistic expectations? Certainly there has to be more to life than this.

Thankfully, there is a way to look at life that will bring peace and joy instead of fear and insecurity. And there is a way to find an everlasting personal worth that never disappoints. We must look at ourselves through the right pair of eyes—God's eyes. He sees us much differently than we do. The problem is that very few of us have ever stopped to discover just what His perspective is. Our days are spent worrying over what neighbors, bosses, teachers, husbands, and even strangers think of us, but we don't pause long enough to consider what the Creator of the universe might have to say about the very same things. Clearly, our priorities are very mixed up.

This brings us to the purpose of the following chapters. We're going to set aside the opinions of our culture, and instead focus upon what God, in His Word, personally says to each one of us. We will look at the most common areas in which we tend to substitute worldly wisdom for godly wisdom. God has a lot to say about the things you and I struggle with every day: perfectionism, people pleasing, physical beauty . . . the list goes on and on. If you have never taken the time to see yourself through God's eyes, I invite you to take a careful look at some truly life-changing topics. We will use an entirely different perspective than the one we've been used to all this time. God's Word is guaranteed to shed new light upon old problems. After all, if human "hindsight is 20/20," imagine how much clearer we will see through the lens of our perfect Creator.

Chapter 2

The Eye of the Beholder
Outer Beauty or
Inner Beauty

There is certainly no shortage of available beauty tips at the Miss USA Pageant. When I was there, the producers had each of us share a beauty secret for the TV audience. Mine was to use slices of cucumber to bring down puffy eyes. There were many more; in fact, there were some I hadn't even heard of. One girl suggested putting baby powder on your scalp if your hair is feeling greasy and there's no time for a shower. Another said that Preparation H (you know what that's for!) works great as a thigh tightener. It's amazing what you can learn from beauty queens!

It's no wonder that pageants are looked at with a skeptically raised eyebrow. Certainly there are more important things for women to think about than greasy scalps and flabby thighs. Or are there? No matter how much rhetoric is given to the equality of women and the strides we have made in the educational and professional worlds, there is still ample evidence that the culture expects women to live up to an unfair physical standard. Women are expected to wear make-up, sport trendy hair styles, and have bodies like the Victoria's Secret catalogue models. Such demands are tough if not impossible.

I'm not here to argue whether the differences between men and women are fair or not, because let's face it—the distinctions are just reality. I hate it that men can be ready in twenty minutes and it takes me an hour. I also can't stand it that gray hair and wrinkles distinguish a man, but the same on women just translates as "old." But with all of the perceived inequality, I'm not quite ready to give up the fun things about being a woman, either. I don't mind nail polish, fashion magazines, jewelry, or any other adornment of womanhood. I like it that the bride gets to wear the beautiful gown and receives all of the attention while the groom remains in the background. Call me old-fashioned, but I'm happy that some differences between the sexes exist.

There is, however, one thing that really bothers me about the gender gap. Somewhere along the line women came under the assumption that the way our faces and bodies look measures how much we are worth as individuals. It's as though we think that the chain of human importance begins with supermodels, drops down to homecoming queens and cheerleaders, and bottoms out with Plain Janes with a few too many inches around the hips. That's wrong . . . completely wrong. Again the problem comes back to whose eyes we are looking through.

The eyes of the culture set up unrealistic expectations, and then demand that we live up to them. Every day when we pick up a magazine, turn on the TV, or look at a billboard we are shown our "ideal." Unfortunately, what we see is air-brushed perfection that virtually no one can attain. Just as we have to be careful that we don't let perfectionism in our work control us, we have to also be concerned that we aren't dominated by what society tells us we should look like. One of the most severe consequences of the perfectionism of looks, triggered by the beauty industry, is the problem of eating disorders. I speak with firsthand knowledge, because the struggle of maintaining bodily perfection is one with which I've had personal experience. Anorexia, which is self-starvation, and bulimia, which involves taking in large quantities of food and then purging the body, are life-threatening behaviors which have physical perfection as their goal.

Famous women such as actress Tracey Gold and gymnasts Nadia Comenici and Cathy Rigby have been open about their struggles with anorexia or bulimia. Certain other notable women, like popular recording artist Karen Carpenter and rising ballerina Heidi Gunther have actually died from complications brought on by eating disorders. Even beloved Princess Diana made it no secret that she daily waged war against bulimia.

It's not just people in the spotlight who struggle

with severe feelings of inadequacy about the way they look. A recent People magazine article revealed that between 8 and 10 million Americans have eating disorders. Furthermore, at least one out of every five women on any given college campus is either anorexic or bulimic. The problem is so prevalent during the college years that I spend a good part of my time traveling to universities around the nation, speaking to collegiate women about the dangers of eating disorders.

When I speak to these women, there is one question I like to ask. It is this—how many women in the United States see pretty models in magazines, perfect bodies on billboards, and gorgeous faces in TV and movies? The answer, of course, is that 100 percent of all women in this country are exposed to some type of cultural pressure to be beautiful. Yet how many women become anorexic or bulimic? The maximum number offered by eating disorder organizations is 21 percent. Not every person who sees the culture's standard for beauty actually feels the need to act upon it in such an extreme way. There must be something that makes the 21 percent go to such lengths in their desire to look perfect. I'll call that distinguishing characteristic "emotional vulnerability."

"Wait a minute," you may be saying. "I don't have an eating disorder, so how does emotional vulnerability apply to me?" Even though you may not starve yourself or binge and purge, you would be a very unusual person to not be affected by society's fashion mandates. TIME magazine reports that 80 percent of all children have been on a diet by the time they reach fourth grade. It's clear that not worrying about the way one looks is the exception rather than the rule. We all struggle with feeling the need to conform to some standard of physical beauty. Whether you're affected by media images a little or a lot, your level of emotional vulnerability will be what determines your reaction to the pressures of the beauty culture. My desire for each person I speak to, and for those who are reading this book, is to offer resources that will diminish your vulnerability and build up your emotional and spiritual defenses to the societal influences that affect every single one of us. Please listen to someone who has been there; the only permanent defense for coping with the overwhelming pressure to be outwardly beautiful is to see beauty from God's perspective. His opinion is dramatically different from the culture's, and I'll take His word over the world's any day.

The Bible is very clear that God's focus is not on the outer person. What He cares about is the inner person. I Samuel 16:7 states, "Man looks at the outward appearance, but the Lord looks at the heart." I also like the way the Living Bible paraphrases God's perspective. The same verse records Him as saying "I don't make decisions the way you do! Men judge by outward appearance, but I look at a [person's] thoughts and intentions."

Reading this verse should completely transform our focus. Believe it or not, I am writing this after one of the all-time greatest hair disasters of my life! Today I went to a new hairdresser to get my summer sun-bleached hair back to its original brown. Little did I know that I would walk out of there with not brown, but orange-red hair! It looks like she and I had a little miscommunication that will take about a month of washing to remedy. That may sound a bit trivial, but everyone knows what it's like to have a bad hair day, and I'll have one for weeks. Needless to say it's very comforting to know that God isn't the least bit interested in how I look on the outside. But since He does care about how I look on the inside, that means I have some heart (not hair) grooming to do! Let's examine how we develop what is truly important to God—inner beauty.

The Bible is full of examples of women that possessed true inner beauty. It's easy to think the Bible is a book about men, but women are represented as well. Some ladies of great inner beauty include Jochebed, Moses' mother; Hannah, Samuel's mother; Debra, a judge of Israel; Phoebe, a deaconess in the early church; and of course Mary, the mother of Jesus. Another incredible example of true inner beauty is found in Proverbs 31, the famous chapter which depicts the qualities which make a woman noble and virtuous. My favorite examples are found in the two books of the Bible which are actually named after women—Esther and Ruth. Not only do these books display some qualities which we should all seek to emulate, but they also make for extremely interesting reading. Esther is the ancient equivalent of a modern day beauty queen, and Ruth stars in one of the most beautiful love stories ever told. Let us look at each of their lives a bit more closely.

Esther's life reads almost like a fairy tale. She comes from a humble Jewish background, but because of incredible outer and inner beauty, finds herself competing with many other women for the position of Queen of Persia. The only judge in this "pageant" was the Persian king, and his vote went to Esther. While reigning as queen, Esther's cousin Mordecai learns that one of the king's advisors is plotting to kill the Jewish people; Esther is the only person who has a chance of stopping his evil plan. Although it means risking her very life, Esther wisely listens to the advice of Mordecai and tactfully appeals to the king to save her people. The king is moved by Esther's plea and demands to know the identity of the man behind the plot. When he hears that his very own advisor is the perpetrator, the king sentences him to death. Queen Esther's courage ultimately delivers the Jewish people, and to this day she is remembered and celebrated at the Jewish Feast of Purim.

Even in this brief synopsis of Esther's life, three character traits of a truly beautiful woman shine through. The first of these inner qualities is a teachable spirit. We see this in Esther's willingness to follow her cousin's advice (Esther 2:10, 4:8-13). We also can read about her teachability when it came to following the counsel of her "pageant coach":

> When it was Esther's turn to go to the king, she accepted the advice of Hegai, the eunuch in charge of the Harem, dressing according to his instructions. (Esther 2:15)

Every time I read this simple little verse, I have no

doubt as to why Esther was chosen Queen. There is something beautiful about a teachable spirit. For the last several years, I have coached young women who have aspired to win pageant titles. Nine times out of ten, the girl who resists constructive criticism doesn't win the crown. On the other hand, the girl who hears advice, thinks it through, and is willing to make changes comes out the winner. It takes a confident person to not be intimidated by instruction, but instead to see it as a way to grow. I like how I Timothy 2:9-11 puts in perspective the difference between mere physical beauty and the inner quality of teachability. This verse states that Christian women should be noticed for being kind and good, not for the way they fix their hair or because of their jewels or fancy clothes. Women should listen and learn quietly and humbly.

A teachable spirit is more important to God than hairstyles and jewelry. It also enhances your relationships with others. The quality of being teachable applies to every area of life: physical, mental, social, and spiritual. If you cultivate this all-important character trait into your inner beauty regime, the effect will be the kind of beauty that actually shines through to the outside. This lets those around you catch a glimpse of who you truly are on the inside.

The next important quality which Esther radiates is self-control. This can be a tough one for me. It's kind of like the old adage: "Lord, grant me self-control . . . and give it to me now!" Though self-control requires work and discipline, it's a necessary component in the portrait of an inwardly beautiful woman. Esther magnifies this self control in numerous instances. First she withholds telling anyone of her Jewish background, as her cousin instructed her to do (Esther 2:20). Then knowing she needs to meet with the king in order to ask for mercy for her people, Esther has the control to spend three days and nights fasting in preparation before entering the king's presence (Esther 4:16). Finally Esther's desire is to disarm the man heading up the wicked plot by having him attend several dinners with her and the king. After controlling herself to not spill the beans, Esther finally acts at the right time. She calmly says to the king, "If I have won your favor, O King, and if it please Your Majesty, save my life and the lives of my people . . . . This wicked man Haman is our enemy!" (Esther 7:3,6). As we can read in the verses that follow, this controlled approach moved the king to grant Esther's request.

Not only does Esther display this wonderful quality, but the book of Titus also lists self-control as one of the most essential traits a woman should possess (Titus 2:3-5). In addition, self-control is listed among the nine fruits of the spirit that all Christians should seek to manifest (Galatians 5:22-23). Just like teachability, we see the importance of self-control in every facet of life. It helps us spend money wisely (skip the malls), eat sensibly (say no to that tempting dessert), and most importantly, make measured decisions and control what words come out of our mouths.

This example of an ancient beauty queen is remarkably relevant to us women of the 21st Century! There is still one more quality which Esther exhibited that just can't be overlooked; it's the attitude of selflessness. Though Esther was queen, she had to follow the rule that no one could approach the king without being invited. The only way an uninvited person would not be put to death for entering the king's presence was if the king chose to hold out his scepter as a welcoming sign. Queen Esther had no idea whether he would do so or not, but that didn't stop her from putting the lives of her people ahead of her own. Before attempting to visit the king, she boldly states to her cousin Mordecai, "Though it is strictly forbidden, I will go in to see the king; and if I perish, I perish" (Esther 4:16).

Those remarkable words make me wonder if I would have the courage to be as selfless as Esther if I were in a similar situation. The truth is, it is unlikely that any of us will be in a position to actually risk our lives to save a nation. However, we have opportunities every day to exhibit selflessness. Taking time out of a busy schedule to help a friend in need is being selfless. Holding our tongue and listening when a husband has had a difficult day is another way of being selfless. The inner quality of selflessness is best described in Philippians 2:3-4.

> Don't be selfish; don't live to make a good impression on others . . . think of others as better than yourself. Don't just think about your own affairs, but be interested in others too, and in what they are doing. (TLB)

A beautiful woman is one who can gaze past her own reflection to see the faces of those around her. The next time you're tempted to put your own agenda ahead of someone else's, remember Esther's example.

A teachable spirit, self-control, and selflessness are all necessary components of the portrait of a truly beautiful woman. Esther gives us a lot to think about, but there is another heroine of the Bible who has lessons to teach us. This particular woman is my favorite. Her name is Ruth, and she certainly exemplifies the meaning of inner beauty. Let's look at her incredible story.

The account begins with a woman named Naomi whose husband and two sons die, leaving her alone with two foreign daughters-in-law. After Naomi tells both young women to let her return unaccompanied to her family home in Judah, one woman chooses to stay with her mother-in-law. That loyal woman, who is willing to give up her culture, people, and all that is familiar to her, is Ruth. Upon arriving in Judah, Ruth suggests that she collect grain at the edge of a field in order to provide food for her and Naomi. Through a series of God-ordained events, Ruth ends up in the field of Naomi's relative—a kind and protective man named Boaz. Following the accepted customs of her culture, Naomi instructs Ruth to ask Boaz to "redeem" her, meaning he would marry Ruth and carry on the name and property of her late husband. Seeing not only a duty to fulfill but also a chance to marry a woman of beautiful character, Boaz goes to tremendous lengths to marry Ruth. In the end, God rewards each person involved by giving Boaz and Ruth a child. This child ultimately becomes the grandfather of the great King David.

Ruth is not as obvious a heroine as is Esther, but that's why I like her. Her beauty is quiet and glows from within. Like Esther, Ruth displays three major character qualities that comprise the beautiful spirit for which God is looking. The first of these traits is loyalty, which is seen numerous times in Ruth's life. One of the most obvious expressions of her loyalty comes in Ruth's decision to stay with her mother-in-law. While this choice could have meant that Ruth would never have another husband or a child and would have to live in a foreign place, Ruth says the following to Naomi:

> "Don't urge me to leave you or to turn back from you. Where you go I will go, and where you stay I will stay. Your people will be my people and your God my God." (Ruth 1:16)

Her loyalty, faithfulness, and kindness did not go unnoticed or unrewarded. When Boaz first learned that Ruth was working on the outskirts of his field, he invited her to work alongside his maids, ensured that no one would harm her, and gave food to her and Naomi. Surprised at Boaz's generosity, the following exchange takes place:

> "How can you be so kind to me?" [Ruth] asked. "You must know I am only a foreigner."

> "Yes, I know," Boaz replied, "and I also know about all the love and kindness you have shown your mother-in-law since the death of your husband, and how you left your father and mother

in your own land and have come here to live among strangers. May the Lord God of Israel . . . bless you for it." (Ruth 1:10-12)

Not only does Ruth receive recognition from Boaz for her loyalty, but she also develops a wonderful reputation in the eyes of those around her. Ruth 3:11 records Boaz as saying, ". . . all my people in the city know that you are a woman of excellence." Could there be a higher compliment? Because of Ruth's example, we see that loyalty is a character quality of a beautiful woman that both God and those around us will notice.

In addition to Ruth's loyalty, her inner beauty is clearly seen in her extremely strong work ethic. In chapter two Ruth takes the initiative to work for herself and Naomi and then proceeds to collect food from morning till night (Ruth 2:2-7). Even more impressive, Ruth comes home after a long day and prepares food for her mother-in-law (Ruth 2:17-18).

I don't know about you, but after I've had a long hard day, I just want to prop my feet up. Yet in this day and age, with women trying to "have it all," relaxing at home is not always an option. It obviously wasn't an option in Ruth's time either. Fortunately God sees a good work ethic as something that reveals a beautiful character. If you read Proverbs 31:10-31, the first thing that stands out in this portrait of a woman is her diligence in working. In fact, verses 13 through 27 are almost exclusively devoted to describing some aspect of her hardworking nature. Even more amazing is the praise that is given to her in the verses that go before and after. She is called an "excellent wife" in verse ten and is said to outshine even the most noble of women in verse 29. That's almost exactly what Boaz says about Ruth in Ruth 3:11.

Now let me be clear. I'm not advocating putting in ridiculous hours at the office, coming home to drown in house work, and then getting four hours of sleep. There needs to be balance, and after the Lord our families must come first. I've used these verses to illustrate that the woman who is full of persistence and is willing to work hard is one who is beautiful in God's eyes. He's not looking for runway models and movie stars. He desires that whatever a woman does, whether it's working outside or inside the home, that it's done with diligence and a willing spirit (Colossians 3:23).

The final quality we will examine in the life of Ruth is one that the Bible says is synonymous with inner beauty. If there were ever a definition of beauty from God's perspective, this is it.

> Your beauty should not come from outward adornment, such as braided hair and the wearing of gold jewelry and fine clothes. Instead, it should be that of your inner self, the unfading beauty of a gentle and quiet spirit, which is of great worth in God's sight. (I Peter 3:3-4)

In Ruth's life the combination of gentleness and quietness yields the sterling trait of humility. Ruth's humility is evident in every recorded major event of her life. We first see humility in her willingness to glean grain at a stranger's field, as this was considered a demeaning job. Furthermore, she refers to herself as a "servant" to Boaz, and yet refuses to be considered even equally as important as Boaz's hired maidservants (Ruth 2:13). Finally, Ruth follows Naomi's instructions and puts herself in the very humbling position of asking Boaz to marry her (Ruth 3:6-9).

It is very important to understand that being humble doesn't mean that we let people walk all over us. Nor does it mean that we must think poorly of ourselves. It simply means we just don't think of ourselves at all! Let me give you a modern-day example of this. I'm sure you can guess that pageants are full of egos. It's very rare to run across a contestant who is beautiful and talented, but doesn't think of herself that way. In all my years of competing and coaching, I never came across such a person until a seventeen year old girl named Danielle came to train with me. Danielle had it all. She was an honors student, a cheerleader, and a student council officer. She also worked as a part-time model for a very prestigious agency. None of this went to her head. She humbly took instruction from me, was kind to all of the contestants around her, and was one of the most down to earth young women I've ever met. The best part of Danielle, however, was that her humility didn't leave her thinking poorly about herself. She had a healthy sense of self-respect, but her world didn't revolve around Danielle. She focused on others and instead of losing herself, she bettered herself. I'm happy to report that Danielle recently won her pageant. And you guessed it . . . she's still as humble as she was before.

Just like Danielle, I'm sure Ruth didn't think of herself as humble. That's the funny thing about humility . . . once you know you've got it, you've lost it! Nevertheless, we can pray that God will help us see ourselves accurately, through His eyes. If we see ourselves as products of remarkable craftsmanship by a great Creator and then allow Him to use us for His glory instead of our own, we will strike the right balance that yields humility. As we're conditioning our minds to move in that direction, we're fortunate to have the example of Ruth.

As we have just read, God's ideas about beauty never change. Six qualities, as seen in the lives of Esther and Ruth, show us what inner beauty is all about. The timeless traits of a teachable spirit, self-control, selflessness, loyalty, humility, and diligence are shown throughout God's Word to be qualities that are precious in His sight. The Bible is clear that outer beauty means nothing, but inner beauty means everything. Proverbs 31:30 states, "Charm is deceitful and beauty is vain, but a woman who fears the Lord, she shall be praised." If we really believe those words, then we will stop focusing on the culture's demands for outer beauty. Instead we'll see that beauty really *is* in the eye of the beholder, and that the only beholder that counts is our Lord.

Chapter 3

When Life Hurts
Tragedy or Triumph

I recently spoke to a young woman I've worked with for months, preparing her for the Miss USA Pageant. Some people might think such competitions don't matter all that much. They probably don't in the grand scheme of things. But to the young woman who had trained like an Olympic athlete, whose blood, sweat, and tears became far more important than the actual crown itself, winning mattered. Winning was her goal. Winning was her dream. She deserved to win. She lost; that's what the defeated voice on the other end told me.

I've come to the conclusion that life is not fair. Far from it, in fact.

My heart hurts right now. It hurts partially because I know this precious girl and wanted her dream to come true. It also hurts because this is far too familiar territory. I may be writing this with a pageant title under my belt, yet I've lost far more than I've won. And it's not just pageants. I've lost relationships. I've lost opportunities. I've lost awards. I know what it feels like when dreams fall by the wayside and when people you love go away. Perhaps you know that feeling, too.

If you're human, you've experienced "the thrill of victory and the agony of defeat." You don't have to be a sports star or a beauty queen to know the truth of that saying. You just have to be breathing. As I have said numerous times, we live in a fallen world. Things aren't perfect, and bad things happen. The question is this: when these painful, unfair things inevitably befall us, what do we do? How should we act? No matter how much self-esteem you have, life is still going to be tough. Let's take a look at how God has equipped us as His treasured children to turn tragedy into triumph.

Of all the women in the Bible who experienced the disappointment, struggles, persistence, and ultimate victory in dealing with life's tragic circumstances, the one who stands out is Naomi. If the book of Ruth were a movie, Ruth would be the lead actress while Naomi would be considered the supporting actress. But her role is no less important in terms of the lesson we can learn from her behavior. Let me summarize the events of Naomi's life as found in the book of Ruth.

Naomi—wife and mother of two sons and two daughters-in-law—lived a life dedicated to God. Very suddenly, Naomi's husband died, and ten years later her sons also died. Having lived her righteous life in a heathen country, Naomi decides to return to her home in Israel. She experiences tremendous sadness and resentment toward God. She even changes her name from Naomi ("pleasant") to Mara ("bitter"). She believes that God has dealt bitterly with her, taking her full life and turning it into an empty one.

Partially because of her daughter-in-law Ruth's resolution to go with her to Israel, Naomi begins to persevere in the midst of her trials. As we read in the last chapter, she arranges the courtship of Ruth and Boaz in order to rebuild the family line of her dead husband and sons. Ultimately, Naomi is rewarded with the marriage of Ruth and Boaz, which produces a grandchild. The book ends with Naomi caring for the little boy, knowing that she is indeed a blessed woman to have a new family to love.

Let's examine several aspects of this story. Like many of us, Naomi starts out thinking life is great. Then tragedy strikes. As you know, sometimes the trial is relatively small, like not getting the job we want or failing to get into the college of your choice. Sometimes the tragedy is devastating, like the death of a loved one, a divorce in the family, or a rape or molestation. Any one of these things—big or small—can turn our world upside down in a heartbeat.

It's at this point that we have the chance to respond—either positively or negatively. In Naomi's case she did what was natural; she grieved. Then she began resenting God, becoming more and more bitter. I'm sure many of us would have done the same thing. However, holding a grudge against God or others ultimately hurts us. It makes us sad and depressed. In fact, we may turn to destructive behaviors—like drugs, alcohol, or an eating disorder—to numb the pain, instead of working through the pain. While this reaction may be natural, normal, and even seem justified, it only creates more havoc in our lives.

I remember a time when I didn't understand what God was doing in my life at all, and I became resentful. You see, like the young lady I mentioned at the beginning of this chapter, I had poured my whole life into competing for a state title within the Miss America Pageant system. I worked countless hours a week, even carrying around a picture of the Miss America crown so that I would never forget my goal. I prayed that God would let me win so that millions of people could hear my voice as a Christian. After all, people take notice of Miss America and what she believes. Finally my competition was at hand. I performed to the best of my ability. I wouldn't have changed a thing. Even strangers told me that the crown was as good as mine. Then they started reading off the names. Fourth runner-up, third runner-up, second-runner-up, first runner-up . . . *first runner-up.* For me, it all stopped there. Instead of winning, I was given that bitter sweet position of "almost, but not quite." It nearly killed me. I couldn't hide my disappointment, try as I might. Someone later told me that when my name was called, I looked like my best friend had just been shot. That's probably a pretty accurate picture. I was in shock and devastated. Tears poured forth as soon as I stepped off stage. My dream had been shattered. What was God thinking?

If only I could have seen through God's eyes at that moment. But I was like Naomi. I couldn't see that God often uses the imperfect circumstances of our lives to develop us into the beautiful persons He wants us to be. He knows how to take bad things and turn them into good (Genesis 50:20). But we have to trust Him. When the hurt is so real and the pain is overwhelming, that is a very hard thing to do.

That's when we must remind ourselves of the truth of God and the sovereignty of His will for our lives. Sovereignty means absolute authority and power. God is supreme. He can do anything at anytime. In fact, He can stop bad things from happening to us—though at times he doesn't. Theologians and scholars have debated the reason for this for years. My belief is that for now, God recognizes evil as a part of this world. Just as He does not force us to love Him, so He does not force people to choose good over bad. We have free will because God created us with a free will. Sadly, our exercise of free will can wind up hurting other people. However, because God is so absolutely powerful, He can use people's evil intentions to ultimately bring about good.

The Biblical story of Joseph illustrates this point perfectly. As a young boy, Joseph was sold into slavery by his jealous brothers. Through a series of circumstances, Joseph obtains favor from the King of Egypt so that he ultimately becomes second in command over the entire country. It was at this time in history that a great famine spread through the entire region. But Egypt, through Joseph's wise planning and counsel, stored up enough food to meet the needs of the Egyptian people through the years of want. Meanwhile, Joseph's brothers were back in Canaan, being hit hard by the famine. Knowing that Egypt had plenty of food, they decided to make the long trek there in hopes of buying some. Upon their arrival, they came face to face with Joseph. When he revealed that he was their long lost brother, they all feared for their lives. Luckily for them, Joseph was in line with God's plan. He was looking through the eyes of a loving Father who could take what started out as a bad situation and make it into something good. Joseph's words to his brothers were: "You intended to harm me, but God intended it for good to accomplish what is now being done, the saving of many lives" (Genesis 50:20).

Joseph realized that his entire family would have died from the famine had he been in Egypt. He knew he was there because of the evil intent of his brothers, but he also knew that God was ultimately in control. God used human evil to bring about a Divine good.

Throughout history and up to this present day, God continues to do this very same thing. In spite of our reaction, God will ultimately do what He wills. The difference to be made is in our attitude. We must decide whether we will trust God's sovereignty and partner with Him, or if we will resent God and turn our backs on Him.

Fortunately our role model Naomi chose to become God's instrument to carry out ultimate good. She masterminded the relationship between Ruth and Boaz, knowing that she could do more than passively sit by and wait for her life to improve. She wisely chose to ensure that her family line would be carried on and that she and Ruth would be taken care of. It's that kind of positive, proactive approach that can make a difference.

It was this approach that "worked" for me after my loss of the crown. I was down for a while. I didn't understand one bit of what God was doing, but I decided there had to be other ways to spread the wonderful message of Jesus to people aside from holding a pageant title. I began taking courses toward my master's degree in Biblical Studies so I would be educated to teach God's Word. Over the course of time, I was encouraged to try out the other major pageant system in the United States—the Miss USA Pageant. I figured, "Why not? What could it hurt?" Amazingly after only a few weeks of preparation, I competed and won the title of Miss Arizona USA. From there I represented my state at the 1998 Miss USA Pageant, made the finals, and shared part of my beliefs on national television. God knew what He was doing all along.

What I learned through my experience is to have faith and be proactive with that faith. The Bible defines faith as something we cannot see (Hebrews 11:6). It's true that we won't see God's hand at work every step of the way, but we can know He is active as we are being active. If you are struggling with an addiction, be proactive and seek help. If you are carrying a grudge against a family member, be proactive and make amends. If you have given up on your dreams, be proactive and go back to school or get back into the race. When we take action, we literally become partners with God, even though we won't always see His plan unfolding.

I'd like to leave you with an analogy to which I have clung whenever I am tempted to believe that my trials will never amount to anything good. It's the story of the weaver's tapestry. When a tapestry is being woven, all that is seen is the underside. Thousands of uneven threads pop through the fabric in all sorts of contorted knots. In a word, it's ugly. But when the weaver is finished and the tapestry is turned over, a beautiful picture is revealed. All of the jumbled threads now form a breathtaking pattern of color. The weaver had the picture in mind all along. But we, the onlookers, needed him to turn it over in order to appreciate the beauty that was there the whole time.

Need I say more? God is weaving a tapestry in your life. The process may appear tangled and unattractive, but the end result is beautiful. After all, it was masterminded by God Himself.

Chapter 4

Waking Up in Someone Else's Dream
Pleasing Others or Pleasing God

Being the night owl that I am, I often stay up late switching back and forth between Jay Leno and David Letterman. Usually I can find an actor or a Top 10 list to entertain me before sleep calls and I leave my late night friends halfway through the show. One night, I couldn't bring myself to turn the TV off. The musical guest had me glued to the screen, as I watched the lovely Faith Hill belt out an upbeat country number for the audience. My heart was pounding, but it wasn't the tune or the rhythm that proved to be responsible; it was the words. Faith was singing about me. The lyrics she sang went like this:

She was Daddy's little girl,
Mama's little angel,
Teacher's pet, pageant queen.

She said "All my life I've been pleasing everyone
but me,
Waking up in someone else's dream."[1]

The words sent chills up and down my spine. I had
never before heard my life summarized in a country-
western "Cliff's Notes" version, but suddenly, as I
watched the Tonight Show, I was made aware of a
tragic truth. A lot of my life had been someone else's
dream.

I remember a time as a teenager when I won a city
pageant. I was so excited. My plan was to go into the
state competition with one idea in mind—to just be
myself. After all, it had worked in the city preliminary.
But then I got a call from one of the people in charge.
She started to pick apart everything about me, from my
clothes to my hair to the song I had chosen to sing. I
hung up sick to my stomach. Someone was trying to
make me the opposite of who I was. She wanted me to
conform to her dream, not mine. It wasn't until years
later, when I heard that Faith Hill song, that I realized
just how many people in similar positions as that
woman had done the very same thing to me throughout my life.

How about you? Are you going to wake up one day
and find that you've been in someone else's dream?
You don't have to be a pageant queen or a teacher's pet
to have this dilemma apply to you. Take a look at the
line in the song where the girl in question realizes that
all her life she's "been pleasing everyone but me."
That's the phrase that screamed the loudest in my ears.

Pleasing everyone but me. That part of the lyrics perfectly describes the trap where so many of us find ourselves. I call it the pitfall of people pleasing. You know you've become prey to this pitfall when, without even realizing it, pleasing others has become your way of keeping peace with others and finding fulfillment in your day-to-day life. Once this unhealthy obsession with people pleasing becomes our way of life, it is only natural to find ourselves struggling every day to please our parents, to keep our husband or our boyfriend happy, and to impress our boss. We find the word "no" has disappeared from our vocabulary. And we realize that our chief end in life is to please the rest of the world, while our own personal identity crashes and burns.

I know that at this point someone is going to be tempted to defend the virtues of people pleasing. Let me make it clear that I am not advocating a complete disregard for other people's feelings. We must be sensitive to the needs and feelings of those around us. However there is a tremendous difference between unhealthy people pleasing and a Christ-like attitude of care and concern for others. Dr. Henry Cloud clarifies and describes the difference as well as the problem:

> We should always be sensitive to others' feelings . . . . But we should never take responsibility for how they feel . . . . Many people have been taught that they are selfish and bad for not being responsible for others' feelings, behaviors, and choices. This teaching keeps codependent behavior going . . . . Our attitudes and beliefs

are our responsibility, not someone else's. Other people's attitudes and beliefs are their responsibility, not ours.[2]

Let's apply this principle of being sensitive to but not being responsible for others' feelings to Faith's song. We see a picture of a young lady who cares so much about keeping everyone around her happy that she never would have dreamed of asserting her own feelings. Maybe she didn't want to be a pageant queen. Maybe she would have preferred to play sports! It's easy for me to imagine what this girl's life might have been like. Let's eavesdrop on a conversation that this young people pleaser might have had with her father regarding her college education.

"Dad, I know we've always planned for me to go to medical school like you did. But with college less than a year away, I've been thinking about majoring in fine arts. You know how I love drawing."

"But Honey, there's no money or future in that. With medical school, you're guaranteed a good paying job. And what about our plans for a father-daughter practice? You're supposed to carry on my legacy! I think this art idea will pass."

This young lady now has the opportunity to respond in two ways. She can either see herself as entirely responsible for living up to her father's expectations and give in, or she can realize that she is not responsible for how he feels and stick to her guns. If you were in her shoes, what would you do?

For years I would have given in if placed in a similar position. I was under the assumption that I was ultimately responsible for other people's feelings. Unfortunately that left me completely out of touch with my own feelings. That's why I know what it's like to be a people pleaser. At the end of this chapter, we'll revisit our case study and see what she decides. For now I'd like to share with you the primary Biblical principle I discovered which finally released me from the pitfall of people pleasing.

There is one overarching theme in the Bible that relates to people pleasing. It can be summed up in the following sentence: We should obey God instead of people. This sounds pretty simple, but unfortunately, this Biblical mandate is often easier said than done. That's why we see the idea reinforced repeatedly. Acts 5:26-32, Galatians 1:10, and I Thessalonians 2:4 all state this clearly. "We must obey God instead of people." When something receives that much attention in Scripture, we should sit up and take notice. Clearly God knew that we would be tempted to place too much emphasis on other people's feelings and opinions. From God's perspective, people pleasing in some cases is equivalent to obeying people. Of course the Bible says that children should obey their parents, but only to the extent that it is right in God's eyes (Ephesians 6:1-2). Parental authority is never greater than God's authority; if a wish of a parent would hurt a child or run contrary to God's will for that child, it should no longer be regarded as the utmost authority. God makes it clear that if one person is obeying another person they must be careful that they are not disobeying God in the process. God knows the danger of people pleasing. He knows that this pitfall carries with it the potential not only to disobey Him, but also to hurt ourselves in the process.

Let's take a closer look at the two consequences of people pleasing. The first is disobeying God. At first glance, it may seem as though people pleasing is something that only hurts us personally. But it also hurts God in that it goes against His plan for our lives. God created us to be unique individuals with a destiny of becoming like Jesus (Romans 8:29). We betray this plan when, as Romans 12:2 puts it, we "let the world squeeze us into its mold" (TLB). To become like Jesus, we must do what the end of the verse says: "Be transformed by the renewing of your mind. Then you will be able to test and approve what God's will is—His good, pleasing, and perfect will." As Dr. Cloud states:

> We are separate people with a separate identity, and we must not be conformed to someone else's wishes that may conflict with what God designed for us. We must own what is our true self, and develop it with God's grace and truth.[3]

If we are living our lives in harmony with God's will, our desire and His desire for our lives will be the same. Consequently, we disobey God when we allow ourselves to wake up in someone else's dream. Any deviation from that amounts to disobedience toward a loving God who only wants the best for us.

It's one thing to be so wrapped up in people pleasing that we fail to obey God's perfect will for our lives.

It's another thing to overtly sin against God in an effort to please others. Think of the boy at a party who does drugs because he is too weak to say no. Think about the girl who lets her boyfriend pressure her into having sex because she doesn't want to disappoint him. These are just two of thousands of examples of people disobeying God because they chose to obey people. The consequences of people pleasing can be extremely serious.

Perhaps the most grave example of disobeying God in order to please people is found in the account of Peter's denial of Christ. Peter was one of Jesus' closest disciples, yet it only took a few questions from some unknown servant girl to cause Peter to betray His Lord and Friend. Take a look at this tragic story.

> Now Peter was sitting out in the courtyard, and a servant girl came to him. "You also were with Jesus of Galilee," she said.

> But he denied it before them all. "I don't know what you're talking about," he said.

> Then he went out to the gateway, where another girl saw him and said to the people there, "This fellow was with Jesus of Nazareth."

> He denied it again, with an oath: "I don't know the man!"

> After a little while, those standing there went up to Peter and said, "Surely you are one of them, for your accent gives you away."

> Then he began to call down curses on himself and he swore to them, "I don't know the man!"

Immediately a rooster crowed. Then Peter remembered the word Jesus had spoken: "Before the rooster crows, you will disown me three times." And he went outside and wept bitterly. (Matthew 26:69-75)

Even though what he did was awful, it's tempting to feel sorry for Peter. Imagine realizing that you just betrayed your best friend because you were too weak to give an unpopular answer. That's what Peter did. He didn't want to be associated with Jesus because he was afraid of what people would think. So he gave into people instead of obeying God, and it only brought him misery.

Therein lies the second consequence of people pleasing—hurting ourselves. Not only do we hurt God when we please people, but we also damage ourselves. We lose our backbone. We diminish the strength of our will. We overextend ourselves. We miss out on the joy of freely giving of ourselves. The list goes on and on. Probably the worst way we hurt ourselves is by coming under the faulty assumption that we have it in our power to make another person happy and fulfilled by doing whatever they want us to do. The next logical assumption that follows is that if we don't do what they want, we will be responsible for their unhappiness. Nothing could be farther from the truth. One person cannot hold the key to another person's happiness. We only have the key to our own. When we let go of the compulsive need to please other people in order to win approval, then we will be on our way to true happiness and we will be in control of our own lives.

How do we free ourselves from the pitfall of people pleasing? It all comes back to the principle of obeying God instead of people. We must filter every encounter we have with another person with this question: "Will doing what this person wants me to do help or hinder my becoming the person God wants me to be?" If the answer is "help", then no problem. If the answer is "hinder", then you must refuse to please the person in question. Note the following example:

Amy had always been active in the church music department. She loved to sing and was gifted at playing the piano. Because she was responsible, the music director would often ask her to do a few "extras". He'd ask her to pick up donuts before Sunday morning service. He'd beg her to stay late after practice to accompany the soloist on the piano. He'd call her late Saturday night and ask her to type the song sheets. None of these were her job, but she felt that to serve the Lord with her talents, she needed to do all that was requested of her. Soon Amy was spending less and less time with her family and more and more time at church. The more burned out she felt, the more she resented her "service." Afraid of displeasing the Lord by ceasing to do "His" work, Amy kept doing whatever the music director asked.

The above story is a classic case of actually disobeying God in the process of serving Him. People do this all the time and don't even realize it! The Lord never intended Amy's willing spirit to be taken advantage of, nor did He intend for her to resent the church and ignore her family. From God's perspective, Amy would be more obedient if she refused to do the things which kept her from being the joyful woman God intended her to be even if that meant cutting back her work at the church. While it's clear to us that Amy should have said "no," Amy's thinking was that it would be wrong to assert herself in this way. Sadly Amy was ensnared in the trap of people pleasing. How much better it would have been if she had set limits on her time so that she could serve the Lord with a cheerful spirit and not neglect herself or her family in the process. If only Amy had asked herself the key question we discussed earlier, "Will doing what this person wants from me help or hinder my becoming the person God wants me to be?" Had she used this filter, her service would have yielded more joy as she set limits on her people pleasing.

With this filter in mind, let's go back to the young lady in Faith's song. In our case study, she is having a discussion with her dad. She wants to go to Art School, but he wants her to go to Medical School. She's under enormous pressure, but she has also decided that she no longer wants to be a people pleaser. She no longer wants to wake up in someone else's dream. Here's what her God-honoring, self-honoring and even parent-honoring response might sound like.

"Dad, I respect the path you've chosen for your life and am grateful for the success and happiness you get from being a doctor. I too want that success and happiness, but I believe the Lord is calling me into the field of fine arts. I don't want to spend my life resenting you for doing something that you want, but I don't want. I know this may be hard for you to hear, but I'm hoping that after some time, you'll be able to accept my decision. I believe it's the right one for me."

As I've said before, I think it's important to have a Biblical role model after whom to pattern your behavior. I'd like to close by showing you a woman in the Bible who refused to give in to people pleasing and instead chose to obey God and to respect herself.

> While Jesus was in Bethany, reclining at the table in the home of Simon the Leper, a woman came with an alabaster jar of very expensive perfume, made of pure nard. She broke the jar and poured the perfume on his head.
>
> Some of those present were saying indignantly to one another, "Why this waste of perfume? It could have been sold for more than a year's wages and the money given to the poor." And they rebuked her harshly.
>
> "Leave her alone," said Jesus. "Why are you bothering her? She has done a beautiful thing to me . . . . I tell you the truth, wherever the gospel is preached throughout the world, what she has done will also be told, in memory of her."
> (Mark 14:3-9)

I can only imagine the mockery and pressure with which this woman was faced. However that was not her concern. Honoring her Lord was all that mattered. Because of her determination to obey God instead of people, she received the distinct honor of having her story told (in more places than just this book) in remembrance of her beautiful and courageous action.

Let's strive to be like this woman who received such honor at the feet of Jesus. Let's strive to live up to the words of Paul in Galatians 1:10 ". . . do I seek to please men? If I still pleased men, I would not be a servant of Christ." Isn't it wonderful that in God's eyes the servant who obeys the Lord instead of people receives the greatest honor?

1. Wiseman, Craig and Bruce, Trey. "Waking up in Someone Else's Dream." Almo Music, 1995.
2. Cloud, Dr. Henry. Changes that Heal, Zondervan Publishing House, 1993, pp. 125, 153, 98
3. Cloud, p. 104

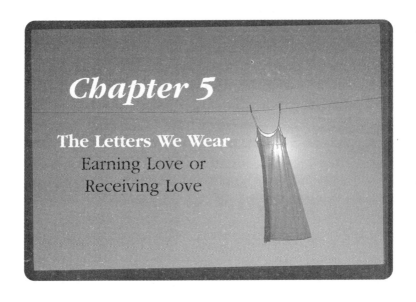

Chapter 5

The Letters We Wear
Earning Love or
Receiving Love

When I was in high school my English class was required to read Nathaniel Hawthorne's *The Scarlet Letter*. While I didn't consider it the most fun reading in the world at that age, it succeeded in making a big enough impact on me that I remember it to this day. The story centers around Hester Prynne, a Puritan woman who finds herself with child from an affair with the town's minister. Because she committed adultery and refused to name the father of the baby, she was forced to wear a big red "A" on her clothing every day of her life as her punishment.

What follows is a powerful story, with a cast of colorful characters and riveting plot twists. While I could write an essay singing the praises of the literary significance of this book, I want to focus on one thing in the story which I think has great application to modern life. Think about the implication of the scarlet letter "A" on Hester Prynne's chest. The fact that she had to wear that symbol for the rest of her life meant that she would always consider herself damaged freight. It also meant that she would never be free to experience genuine forgiveness and a release from guilt and shame. Without those, it is very difficult to ever know genuine love. I think it's safe to assume that if Hester were a real-life person, she would seriously question God's love and whether she could ever know it.

I think a lot of us go through life feeling like we have a big letter on our chests from negative past experiences. Your "A" may stand for abuse. Perhaps you walk around with a big "I" for inferiority. Or maybe you think you deserve a big "U" on your chest—for unforgiven. Whatever the letter on your chest says, chances are you are trying to make up for it in some way. Think about it. We just studied about the compulsion so many of us have to try to please others. We do that because we are trying to prove that we deserve love. But as we are about to learn, love is something that can't be earned; it must be freely given.

The truth of the matter is that we are human and we make mistakes. Moreover, other people can be evil and can do us wrong. Whether it's sin of our own accord or the cruelty of others that makes you feel like you are unworthy of love, one thing is certain. God never intended you to bear the burden of a scarlet letter. He wants to release you from any guilt, shame, or false feelings of unworthiness. He wants you to be free to know His love and to realize how very special you are in His eyes. Until we are able to see ourselves as totally loved and accepted by God, we will walk around like Hester, ever reminded that we are unworthy of love. What a miserable way to live! The last thing in the world that God wants is for you to let things in the past stand in the way of experiencing His love in the present.

Let's try to understand why it's so easy to feel like damaged freight. Then we'll be able to press ahead toward recognizing and living out the reality of God's love for us on a daily basis. The core problem is not a lack of intellectual knowledge about God's love. Even children learn in Sunday School that "Jesus loves me." The problem is that we fail to take that head knowledge and turn it into heart knowledge. It's not enough to know that Jesus loves you, your heart needs to understand the depth of what that love truly means.

Whenever I want my emotions to grasp something my mind understands but my heart doesn't, I translate the truth from words into a picture. I visualize the truth through images—found in either a story, a song, or something artistic. I'm no scientist, but I am knowledgeable enough about scientific research to know that the factual left brain, combined with the artistic right brain makes the biggest impact on our psyche. To further illustrate the love of Christ, let's look at a Bible story that paints the picture of His love, freely given in spite of our frailties and errors. Ironically, this story is the Biblical version of *The Scarlet Letter*—but with a much different ending.

But Jesus went to the Mount of Olives. At dawn He appeared again in the temple courts, where all the people gathered around Him, and He sat down to teach them. The teachers of the law and the Pharisees brought in a woman caught in adultery. They made her stand before the group and said to Jesus, "Teacher, this woman was caught in the act of adultery. In the Law Moses commanded us to stone such women. Now what do you say?"

But Jesus bent down and started to write on the ground with His finger. When they kept on questioning him, He straightened up and said to them, "If any one of you is without sin, let Him be the first to throw a stone at her." Again He stooped down and wrote on the ground.

At this, those who heard began to go away one at a time, the older ones first, until only Jesus was left with the woman still standing there. Jesus straightened up and asked her, "Woman, where are they? Has no one condemned you?"

"No one sir," she said.

"Then neither do I condemn you," Jesus declared. "Go now and leave your life of sin." (John 8:1-11)

Jesus' words are incredible. "*Neither do I condemn you.*" Here's a woman actually caught in the middle of committing adultery, a sin worthy of death in the Mosaic Law. She wasn't just telling a fib or gossiping a little . . . she was really in trouble. But unlike the people of Hester Prynne's day, Jesus didn't want to mark her with an "A." Rather He wanted to show His love through forgiving her and not holding her sin against her. He wanted to enable her to clean up her act, but He wasn't going to hold her in a grip of guilt and shame until she did. Her forgiveness in His eyes was immediate, final, irrevocable.

That same matchless grace and forgiveness applies to you and me. Can you put yourself in that woman's shoes and hear the voice of Jesus freeing you from condemnation? The Bible explains that once a person becomes a Christian, he or she is reconciled to God through Jesus. This means our relationship with Him is forever changed. Romans 8:1-2 echos Jesus' words to the woman caught in adultery and explains our standing before God: "There is now no condemnation for those who are in Christ Jesus because through Christ Jesus the law of the Spirit of life set me free from the law of sin and death."

Again, we are reminded that we are not condemned. We are not guilty in God's eyes. Before we were Christians, we were God's enemies, but all that is changed because of Jesus. Now we are His friends, free from accusation and completely without blemish (John 15:15, Colossians 1:21-22). When God sees us, He sees pure white. He sees nothing but a dearly loved, new creation (II Corinthians 5:17). When God looks at us, and we have asked for forgiveness, He no longer sees our bad choices of yesterday or even the junk of today. He sees none of it. All He sees is Jesus—because on the cross, Jesus permanently took our place.

In spite of this truth, we still think at times that we are unloved by God. It is hard to accept this unconditional love. Because I am so performance oriented, I feel worthy of God's love when I'm reading the Bible or doing something generous and kind. However, the minute my attitude is bad or I say something critical, it's easy for me to start believing that God no longer loves me as much as He did before. When I spell it out like that, I see how silly I am to believe that God would operate that way. But at the same time, I see from where my problem stems. The problem of thinking that God's love fluctuates with our behavior is directly related to thinking God's love can be earned in the first place. We can never be worthy of the love of a holy and righteous God. Therefore I am no closer to being loved by God when I am praying than when I am sinning. Certainly God is glorified when I do what is right, and He is dishonored when I do what is wrong. But His love is the same from one minute to the next.

Imagine the parent of a little baby. That baby can do nothing but cry, eat and totally depend upon her mommy and daddy. The little baby hasn't earned their love by any action on her part. Do you think those parents love that baby any more when it is quiet instead of crying? Of course not. The baby is loved just because she is their child. Similarly we are God's children, adopted into His family (Ephesians 1:5-6). God is our Father and we are co-heirs with Jesus Christ, in a position to experience all of the benefits to which He is entitled (Romans 8:14-17, Galatians 4:6-7). There is no good thing that God, as our loving Father, does not wish to give us.

This may be hard for you to understand if your relationship with your earthly father or mother was strained or abusive. If you did not experience love from your biological parents, then accepting God's unconditional love will be more difficult for you. Remember—the Bible says that we are adopted into God's family. When parents adopt a child, they choose that child; they want that child. In the same way, God adopted you because He so desperately wanted you. I know families who wait years to adopt a child, and when they are finally handed that baby, their love overflows. It's so strong a love that you can almost see it. They've been storing up love for the baby for whom they've been waiting. From the beginning of time God has stored up His love for you—the child He chose. Now that you are His, He can't wait to pour forth His never-ending love on you.

As we review this chapter, we see that each of us starts out like Hester Prynne or the woman in the Bible caught in adultery. No one is questioning that they deserve a scarlet letter, just as we all deserve to be marked by our sin. But when we open our hearts to Jesus, He steps in and moves us from being God's adversary to His friend. It doesn't stop there. We are more than just friends of God; as Christians, we are His special children. Just as good parents would never want their children to feel as though they had to earn the love of their mother or father, so God wants us to be released from that burden. He wants us to run to and accept the love that He so longs to give.

As we draw to a close, I'd like you to find a quiet place. Take a moment to be by yourself with no inter-ruptions. Read the following words taken from the book *Longing for Love* by Ruth Senter. Don't let them stop at your head; let them sink all the way into your heart.

> Relax, my child. I am the one who knows you best and also the one who knows you most. You were loved from eternity past, even before I brought you to life in your mother's womb. All the days ordained for you were written in my book before one of them came to be . . . . Remember that you are part of a flawed world. This is what my love is all about—to love you in your flawed condition. Because I am rich in love, I made you alive while you were still dead. Some people will die for good people. I died before you were good—while you were still a sinner. It was not my way to ask you to be lov-ing before I could love you. And it is not my way to ask you to be loving in order for me to continue loving you. Your world makes pro-mises based on how you will respond. I love you regardless of your response. Your world changes people, then loves them. I love you first, and along the way, because you are loved, you are changed."[1]

The world makes you earn love. God just wants to give it. I'll take God's gift any day. How about you?

1. Ruth Senter, <u>Longing for Love</u>, Bethany House, 1997, pp. 25-27

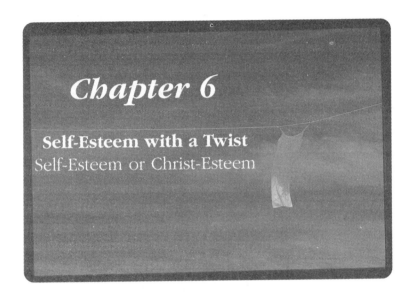

Chapter 6

Self-Esteem with a Twist
Self-Esteem or Christ-Esteem

Self-esteem has really become a buzz word in today's society. Whenever you turn on the news you hear some study about the importance of self-esteem and how if everyone just had a little more of it, the world would be a better place.

If you've ever seen the MTV show *The Real World*, then you know what I'm talking about. Since the show basically chronicles the lives of real people—not actors—they always choose interesting characters with just enough dysfunction in their lives to make them intriguing to watch. It never fails that when one of these people have a crisis needing resolution, another member of the show will challenge the distraught friend to "believe in himself," or to "be strong in herself." Basically, the friends are advocating the concept of self-esteem. But what exactly is self-esteem and how does one obtain it?

I'd like to discuss this concept and how it relates to the principles in this book. On the surface, you might conclude that everything I have been talking about deals with the idea of self-esteem. That's true in a way. However, I believe a closer look will reveal that seeing our image through God's eyes puts an entirely new spin on the ever popular notion of self-esteem.

The best definition of self-esteem that I found is having pride in one's self. In spite of the negative connotations that the word pride receives, having some self-pride doesn't seem like that bad of an idea. After all, if we thought a little more of ourselves we wouldn't be so quick to think that our lives lack meaning and purpose. Nor would we feel the compulsion to be perfect and please people so much of the time. We certainly wouldn't have trouble believing that we are worthy of love.

Apparently "getting a little more self-esteem" must be easier said than done. After all, you probably wouldn't be reading this book if self-pride could be attained overnight!

I believe there are two main reasons why people struggle to develop self-esteem. The first is pretty obvious: bad things happen to good people, and those things eat away at our image of ourselves. For example, I have a friend who was sexually molested as a child. This caused her to grow up feeling guilty and ashamed. She didn't believe she was worthy of genuine love. She used food as a comfort and gained a lot of weight. This led to more feelings of shame because she didn't fit society's definition of the perfect girl with the perfect body. What began as someone's evil action against her ended up deeply affecting her thoughts, feelings, and behavior patterns. This in turn led to an ever-growing sense of self-hatred, the exact opposite of self-pride or self-esteem.

Too many women are like my friend. Events happen and choices are made which cause a downward emotional spiral, bringing their self-esteem lower and lower. It's no wonder that women are hurting. If this weren't bad enough, there is an even more profound reason why people aren't naturals at developing self-esteem. This goes back to the fact that we live in a fallen world. In the beginning, people lived in perfection, having been created in the image of God. I'm sure having self-esteem was easy then. However, the entrance of sin into the world has corrupted all things—including us. Our image has been tarnished. Fortunately, Jesus died on the cross to restore the image that was once destroyed. The problem is that we're not living as though that negative image was destroyed, nor are we living like we have a new image in God's eyes. Unfortunately, all the baggage of yesterday comes along with us when we become Christians. Until we train our minds to think of ourselves as new creations with a brand new image in God's sight, we will never develop self-esteem. That's where we got off track in the first place. In reality we don't need to acquire more self-esteem at all. What we really need to develop is something that I call Christ-esteem.

You may be wondering, "What is Christ-esteem and what happened to self-esteem?" Well, it's really simple. Having pride in one's self might sound good, but the Bible says the rules regarding self-image are different for Christians. Once we become believers in Christ we experience a spiritual rebirth (John 3:3), we become new creations (II Corinthians 5:17), and we "no longer live, but Christ lives in us" (Galatians 2:20). In other words, our original "self" has been replaced by a new self, defined only by the goodness of Christ. Therefore, any esteem or pride we have should be in Christ. In a very literal way it is more fitting to have Christ-esteem rather than self-esteem.

If we are Christians, we already have the potential to live our lives full of Christ-esteem. So how do we activate this in our day to day thoughts and activities? Two verses should be kept in mind as foundational for making Christ-esteem real in our lives. Let's take a look at both.

The first is II Corinthians 10:17 which simply states, "Let him who boasts boast in the Lord." This verse is the summation of the whole idea of having Christ-esteem, for it reminds us that apart from who we are in Christ, we have nothing. With Christ everything we do reflects the new image that God gave to us. Thus, everything we do in Christ has newfound meaning and worth, and we in turn develop significance.

The second verse to remember regarding Christ-esteem is found in Ephesians 1:9. It says, ". . . He made us accepted in the Beloved." Break that down: He made us accepted. Don't you love that? Many of us go through life feeling unaccepted, unworthy and inferior. But God makes us acceptable through the "Beloved"— His Son, Jesus Christ.

When I was in high school, I felt very unaccepted. I didn't feel pretty enough. I didn't feel cool or popular enough. I dreaded going to school because I was so scared of what other people would think of me. I was sure that I was going to do something stupid and wind up the laughing stock of my school. Not too long ago, my husband and I walked the halls of my old school, just for memory's sake. What a difference I felt! I wasn't afraid; I was confident! I felt I could run into any of those people from the past and feel good about myself. Had I changed? No. I'm still the same person I was then with a few more years and experiences under my belt. But had my perspective changed? You bet. I view myself in an entirely different way today than I did then. I view myself as accepted, not unaccepted. I find that acceptance in God's eyes.

My question is this—why wait? You are accepted right now, in the Beloved. You are precious to God. You are a unique creation. You have every reason to have pride in yourself . . . not because of anything you've done, but because of who you are. You are God's loved and treasured child. Nothing you could ever do could make you more accepted in His sight than you are right now. That is the truth of Christ-esteem.

Now ladies, I have tried to present you with Biblical

role models for each new concept we've addressed. But I have to admit that this concept of Christ-esteem is best exemplified by a man in the Bible. So I must break with our theme and ask you to join me in looking at the life of a man—the apostle Paul. He knew what Christ-esteem versus self-esteem was. Read the following Scripture and you'll learn more of "Christ-esteem."

> The ones who worship by the Spirit of God, exult in Christ Jesus, and do not rely on human credentials—though mine too are significant. If someone thinks he has good reasons to put confidence in human credentials, I have more: I was circumcised on the eighth day, from the people of Israel and the tribe of Benjamin, a Hebrew of Hebrews. I lived according to the law as a Pharisee. In my zeal for God I persecuted the church. According to the righteousness stipulated in the law I was blameless. But these assets I have come to regard as liabilities because of Christ. More than that, I now regard all things as liabilities compared to the far greater value of knowing Christ Jesus my Lord, for whom I have suffered the loss of all things—indeed, I regard them as dung—that I might gain Christ, and be found in Him, not because of having my own righteousness derived from the law, but because of having the righteousness that comes by way of Christ's faithfulness—a righteousness from God that is in fact based on Christ's faithfulness. (Philippians 3:4-9, NET)

Let's analyze what Paul is saying. In this well known passage in Philippians, Paul admits that he has every reason to have self-esteem because of his religious heritage and practices. He confesses, however, that these things are liabilities or actual disadvantages when compared to knowing Christ. In other words, Paul realizes that his own self-esteem had the potential to get in the way of his genuine Christ-esteem . . . which is of far greater value and worth. In fact, Paul calls the things he achieved "dung" or "rubbish." Paul doesn't mean that personal achievements are evil, rather, he is saying that compared to the blessings that come from being a follower of Christ, the two are not even comparable!

Let me close by telling you a story of Christ-esteem that is very close to my heart. It's about a girl I'll call Trish. Trish was one of the countless women to whom "bad things" were done. She tried everything in her power to be perfect and gain love from those around her. She inevitably failed. As a result, Trish developed anorexia in an attempt to be perfectly thin. Needless to say, her anorexia hurt her worse and her self-esteem hit rock bottom. Trish knew she needed to find a way out, but all of the self-help books and programs she tried failed. Every approach people suggested to cure her of her anorexia and boost her self-image fell short. Then one day her sister gave her a little workbook on eating disorder recovery through a relationship with Christ. As Trish read the book and learned about what it meant to be loved by God, she started developing Christ-esteem. She in turn felt better about her self-esteem, because now the two were the same thing. Trish was eventually healed from her eating disorder and is now involved in full-time Christian work.

Meeting Trish was one of the highlights of my life, not only because I went through the exact same struggles, but also because that "little workbook" was written by me! How honored I am to be the one God chose to share the principles of Christ-esteem with Trish.

Ladies, if you are trying in vain to develop self-esteem, strive no longer. Instead remember to take pride in what the Lord does through you. Never forget that you are one hundred percent accepted by God because of Christ. That is the wonderful reality of Christ-esteem.

Maybe the world would be a better place if everyone had a little more self-esteem. But if everyone had Christ-esteem, it would be more than just a better place—it would be heavenly. And one day, it will be.

Chapter 7

Damsels In Distress No More!
Being Half or Being Whole

When I was in high school, I experienced my first crush. Was it ever a doozy! It caused me to do all sorts of strange things, including late night drive-bys of the boy's house. But all of my antics proved to be for nothing when I found out that he had asked my best friend to the school dance. Talk about a broken heart!

Recently I ran across some hilarious comments about relationships straight out of the mouths of babes. Take a look at these wild answers.

Question: What do most people do on a date?

Answer: Dates are for having fun and people should use them to get to know each other. Even boys have something to say if you listen long enough. —Lynnette, age 8

Question: Is it better to be single or married?

Answer: It's better for girls to be single, but not boys. Boys need someone to clean up after them. —Anita, age 9

And my favorite . . .

Question: How do you decide who to marry?

Answer: You got to find somebody who likes the same stuff. Like, if you like sports, she should like it that you like sports, and she should keep the chips and dip coming.
—Alan, age 10

These children's innocent perspectives of marriage are priceless, but it's clear that relationships require some deeper thinking. While I'm sure our attitudes about marriage and dating have matured since we were children, we probably still need to make sure that our current thinking is in line with God's perspective.

A few years ago, I saw the movie "Jerry Maguire." In it was a line that, at the time, I thought was extremely romantic. It has Jerry—played by the dashing Tom Cruise—confess this to the woman he loves, "You complete me." Doesn't that sound pretty? Wouldn't you just love to hear those words? I was convinced that such words would rock my world if anyone would ever say them to me. But the more I thought about the line over the next few weeks, I realized the thought behind those words is rather deceiving. The whole idea of one person needing another person to "complete" them is not a healthy starting point for a relationship. Tragically, a lot of women are looking for just that . . .

someone to complete them. Someone to make them feel whole. For whatever reason, they are too timid or weak to persevere in personal completeness, so they look to someone else to do it for them. The truth is that such an approach always backfires.

I am convinced that the number-one reason that women are unhappy in relationships is that they enter into a relationship in order to secure some sort of self-worth. Instead of being a complete person on their own and then looking for Mr. Right, they conclude that they only will be complete when they find Mr. Right. It's the "Jerry Maguire" trap!

Read what popular talk-show host Dr. Laura Schlessinger says in her aptly named book, *Ten Stupid Things Women Do to Mess Up Their Lives.*

> Think of it like this: If you bring your own goals and dreams and self-awareness to a marriage, the other person can be a tremendous source of comfort and support when your career or one of your friendships is going through a rough patch. That's true for anything that causes your ego to suffer a blow—and you can and should do the same for your partner.
>
> If you bring to the relationship nothing but your neediness, the balance is all off. You become your husband's baby, his perpetual "damsel in distress." Though a damsel may be macho-assuaging for a while, it is not long before she becomes a constant emotional drain and a total "taker."

In such a lopsided situation, you're bound to feel lonely, because feelings of self-worth do not come from the mere existence or presence of someone in your life. Counting on that, in fact, just makes the pain of your sense of personal nothingness even worse.[1]

Ring any bells? It sure does for me. I have to admit that for years I looked to men to give me a sense of worth. Consequently I let them mistreat me verbally, play terrible games with my emotions, and treat me like dirt just to hold on to someone—anyone—who would "love" me. I know full well today that what those guys did to me was anything but loving. But I have to partially blame myself for being too weak to stand up for the treatment a woman deserves. Only when I stopped looking to men for self worth and began to develop my Christ-esteem did I set myself free of bad relationships. It took years, but ultimately I discovered that as God's daughter, I was worthy of a prince who would treat me like the princess of the King that I truly am in Christ.

My hope is that you will come to that same realization as well. I want you to value yourself so much that you refuse to settle for anything less than God's best for you. The only way you will ever reach that place is if you take Christ-esteem and use that as a springboard in becoming the woman you want to be (and God wants you to be) when you one day walk down the aisle. Remember this: You are complete in Christ. That wholeness means you are equipped to do great things, to dream big dreams, to work hard, to develop your character, and to give of yourself to others around you.

Let's look at a Biblical example of such a woman.

In the most beautiful, romantic book of the Bible, "The Song of Solomon," we are introduced to a woman called "The Shulamite." The Shulamite is believed by many Bible scholars to be King Solomon's first and truest love. The book is primarily a dialogue between Solomon and this young woman he loves, beginning with their courtship and ending during their married life. As a result, this section of the Bible serves as a wonderful handbook on how a man and woman should view each other and treat each other. Because of this, we get a glimpse as to how we should behave if we are to date, marry, and live as wives the way God intended. Here are just a few features of the Shulamite that we should seek to emulate as communicated to us through the words of King Solomon.

In Hebrew culture, things such as animals, plants, and flowers were used to symbolically depict certain characteristics. Beginning in the first chapter, Solomon compares his beloved to his filly among the chariots of Pharaoh. I'm sure women today would not appreciate being likened to a horse, but it really was quite a compliment in Solomon's day. Only the best horses pulled the king's chariot; they were the finest and strongest. Immediately, we see that a woman of God is strong and of excellent caliber; she is set apart from other women. From there, Solomon says that his beloved's eyes are like doves. This tells us of the Shulamite's purity, as a dove personified innocence. Thus pureness of heart and behavior is to be pursued.

In chapter 2 verse 2, Solomon says, "Like a lily

among thorns, so is my love among the daughters." This single verse is so telling. It lets us know that a Godly woman, with stellar character, is hard to find. The king's Shulamite bride is unique for she possesses the qualities that most women do not try to develop. Other women are thorns, but she is a beautiful flower.

Finally, we learn one of the most necessary traits necessary for being complete in a relationship. This time we hear it from the mouth of the Shulamite herself. She says in Song of Solomon 1:6, "Do not look upon me, because I am dark, because the sun has tanned me. My mother's sons . . . made me the keeper of the vineyards, but my own vineyard I have not kept" (NKJV). We see that the Shulamite has dark skin because she has been working outdoors, in contrast to the fair-skinned women of leisure. Because she worked so hard in the fields, out of respect for her family's wishes, she was forced to put her physical appearance second to her work. This tells us volumes. This woman is respectful to authority, a motivated worker, and not vain about her looks. All of these are qualities of a woman of God, and consequently make a woman attractive to a genuine man of God.

I encourage you to read all of the book of Song of Solomon. In it you will discover just how beautiful the king considers this woman to be. It encourages me that Godly character does more to increase my physical beauty than any workout program, make-up or hair product ever could. Truly the right man is attracted by the right things.

Let's defer once again to Dr. Laura, who describes

what quality men are looking for in a relationship: "It's true that the good guys out there do want a total woman . . . a centered, self-aware human being who wants to, rather than needs to, be with him as a companion, lover, friend, co-parent." There is the key. Did you catch it? The woman wants to, rather than needs to, be with him. Only a woman with genuine Christ-esteem who is actively pursuing Godly character—like the Shulamite—will have the inner strength to not need a man to complete her. On the contrary, because she is a whole person, she will seek a whole person. The beauty of this is that two complete people have an amazing capacity to truly become one. They will be two distinct persons, with one unique purpose: becoming who God intended them both to be and encouraging each other in that process.

What can you do to put this theory into practice? Let me suggest two things. First, make a pledge to yourself. Determine that you will become the person you are looking for. Does that make sense? Let me explain. Instead of pining away for a kind man with a gentle heart who loves God and works hard, you become a kind woman with a gentle heart who loves God and works hard. In other words, every quality you want in the "perfect man" must first be exemplified in your own character and behavior. After all, why would such a "perfect" man want someone who was not his relative equal?

The second suggestion I have helps to make the first suggestion even more practical and tangible. Make a list. I called mine my "Top Ten List" (remember, I'm a David Letterman fan). I searched my heart to discover ten qualities that were non-negotiable traits that my future husband would have to have. The things on my list were:

1) Being a committed Christian
2) Having integrity
3) Being kind-hearted
4) Being a motivated, hard worker
5) Having good communication skills
6) Having similar family backgrounds
7) Being a true gentleman
8) Having similar views about children
9) Having a compatible sense of humor
10) Being attractive to me (I specifically added those two little words to the end to remind me that my opinion—not anyone else's—mattered!)

Yours may be the same or completely different. Regardless, if these ten things are truly important, then you are creating a standard for both yourself and your future spouse. Remember, you should strive to be all of the things you want your mate to be.

For several years, I met men who had seven or eight of the qualities I desired. But something was always missing. Even when in my weaker moments I wanted to dismiss the Top Ten List, my gut instinct wouldn't let me. I wasn't genuinely satisfied, and I had developed enough Christ-esteem not to settle for anything less than what I had prayerfully determined was God's best for me.

Just about the time I had completely forgotten the list and was off pursuing my own goals and dreams, along came someone special. We quickly became good friends. The more time I spent with him, the more I saw all ten qualities emerge. This was the first person ever to possess these qualities who I could honestly say I felt a spark for at the same time! I didn't have to manipulate the list or my feelings for him. About two years after our first meeting we were engaged, and a year later we were married.

I am blessed to have married a quality man who did exactly what I did. He developed a list—only in his case called it a "silhouette"—of what he wanted his wife to be like. And you know what? This Godly man didn't have very rigid qualifications for physical beauty, but he did have quite a high standard for beauty of the heart. I truly believe that any man worth your time will agree with my husband's perspective on inner versus outer beauty. As we discussed in a previous chapter, there's no question that God, men, other women, and the world around us need beautiful women of character much more than they need a pretty face.

I wish I could outline every possible suggestion for securing a happy and successful relationship. After all, thousands of books have been written on the subject and we've just touched on a few concepts in these pages. But I want to reiterate the overriding principle that you should have as "true North" on your relationship compass. Don't look to someone else to complete you. You be complete in Christ and in yourself. Hold yourself to the same standards you desire in another and always remember that God's daughter is not a damsel in distress, she is a princess . . . deserving of a prince.

1. Schlessinger, L.C. <u>Ten Stupid Things Women do to Mess up Their Lives.</u>, Harper, 1995, p. 9

Chapter 8

Why Wait?
Worry or Waiting

Aside from carpal tunnel syndrome, I suppose there is one major drawback to the task of writing a book like this—it forces you to bear your soul. In reading these pages, you have seen the deepest parts of me. You have learned of my struggles with self-image and my tendency to compare myself to other women. You've also read of my deep need for love and approval which caused me to fall into the traps of per-fectionism and people pleasing. And you've even seen that I have battled the awful syndrome of anorexia.

Now I have another thing to add to the list. I have a horrible tendency to worry. Not just worry a little, but sometimes worry to the point of panic attacks. There have been times when I've been so fraught with worry that I have cried and trembled with fear, dreading that which I could not control. Though I'm getting better at managing it, worry is still a major force in my life with which I must reckon.

About a year ago I was faced with a horrifying prospect. I was graduating with a Master's degree and had no job options whatsoever. To make matters worse, I didn't even know what I really wanted to do. I knew I wanted to minister to women. I knew I wanted to be involved in spreading the gospel and nurturing people in their relationship with God. I also knew that my most effective way of doing that was through public speaking. But what kind of jobs are out there like that? None that I could think of! I knew of no place I could go, submit an application, and become a nurturing, encouraging speaker to women. My career goal seemed hopeless, straight out of left field. I tried compromising by applying for church staff positions. No luck. I tried to join a campus ministry to work with college girls. Again, no luck. Finally I just started offering my services as a volunteer, and no one even took me up on that!

Needless to say, I began to lose it. My feelings about my worth as a human being plummeted. I truly began to believe that my life was going to amount to nothing, and that my purpose on this earth was futile. I panicked and fell into major depression. All of the Christ-esteem I thought I possessed vanished. I was caught deep in the trenches of worry and couldn't find a way out.

Have you ever worried about the future, over things you couldn't see? Earlier in the book we discussed that faith is defined as being "certain of what we do not see" (Hebrews 11:6). This verse leads me to a conclusion—the antidote to worry must be faith. Unfortunately when you're in a difficult relationship, or you've just lost your job, or you haven't a clue as to how to make a tough life decision, faith is the last thing you're probably thinking about. And so you worry. The Bible says in Matthew 6:25-34 that worrying is the most futile thing we could do. It can't accomplish one single thing. Yet we all do it, even to the point of self-destruction. If we are ever going to get our tendency to be anxious replaced with contentment and peace, we must learn how to use faith to combat worry.

There are two women in the Bible who were faced with serious life dilemmas that had the ability to produce worry in their hearts. Their names are Sarah and Hannah, and their problem was barrenness. In Jewish culture, not being able to have a child was like the kiss of death. Just as we in 21st Century America often gage our self-worth by what we accomplish or achieve, so a Hebrew woman's worth was measured by the children she produced.

These two women are both hailed in the Bible as women who, in the grand scheme of things, displayed tremendous amounts of faith. In fact, Sarah is talked about more in Scripture than any other woman and is mentioned specifically for her faith in Hebrews 11. Hannah also exemplifies incredible trust in the Lord. There is a difference in the way that these two women lived out their faith, however. They are distinct in that one woman had faith from the start and the other woman wasted precious time and energy worrying. By looking at their lives and responses, we will see two distinct ways of handling worry. One requires looking through God's eyes, while the other forgets that there exists a better perspective.

Let's begin with Sarah's story, found in the book of Genesis. She was in an awkward position. God had promised her husband Abraham that he would become the father of a mighty nation, but if she could produce no children, how was this to be accomplished? This led Sarah to—you guessed it—worry. She responded to her anxiety over how God's plan was to be fulfilled by taking matters into her own hands. She decided to give her maid to Abraham, so that he could have a child with her. This act alone caused many problems. All sorts of jealousies developed and Sarah resented the son of her maid and ultimately the maid was banished. Because of Sarah's refusal to wait on God to fix her dilemma, a family experienced tremendous strife. In addition, a new nation was born of Sarah's maid that is at odds with Abraham and Sarah's people, the Israelites, to this very day.

If only Sarah had employed faith and waited for God to act. Psalm 37:3-8 explains why waiting on God is always the best response. Read these incredible words.

> Trust in the Lord . . . . Delight yourself also in the Lord, and He shall give you the desires of your heart. Commit your way to the Lord, trust also in Him, and He shall bring it to pass . . . . Rest in the Lord, and wait patiently for Him . . .

Do not fret—it only causes harm. (NKJV)

That's right! Fretting only causes harm. I know that from firsthand experience. When I worried about my future, when I refused to have faith that the Lord would use me the way He wanted, I entered into all sorts of problems. Not only was I depressed and anxious, but I started down career paths that were totally against God's will for me. They were not immoral job choices, but they were not God's best. Whenever I took steps in such directions, calamity would inevitably follow. Taking things into my own hands was not working. Once again I fell into a deep depression, doubting my personal worth and even questioning God's plan for my life.

This brings us to Hannah. Do I ever wish I had responded as she did when faced with a legitimate cause to worry. Her situation was a little different from Sarah's in that she wasn't trying to raise up a nation with her children, but she was attempting to compete with her husband's other wife who had no problem bearing children. The other wife was provoking Hannah constantly, teasing her to the point where Hannah started slipping into depression. She ended up crying so much she couldn't even bring herself to eat. But that's where it ended for Hannah. She determined not to live in worry. Instead, she prayed fervently, asking God to give her a child. She promised to raise him as one consecrated to God from birth. After doing this, the Bible says that she "went her way and ate, and her face was no longer sad" (I Samuel 1:18).

By faith Hannah trusted that God would honor her prayer. She didn't know how long it would take, but she knew she had done all she could do. Her job now was to wait upon the Lord and trust Him. And sure enough, before long, Hannah gave birth to a son.

Hannah seems to have only had to wait a matter of months; Sarah had to wait until her old age to see the son God promised her. Hannah acted in faith immediately; Sarah took a few more years to believe God's promise. God gave them each a child, because as we know, God's will always prevails. The difference is found only in the amount of time that was wasted worrying.

Looking back it seems I spent at least two months in non-stop worry. Slowly but surely, I started reading my Bible and writing prayers to the Lord in my journal. When I felt too sad to do either, I listened to Christian music, allowing the message of the lyrics to seep into my heart. I was reminded of a powerful Scripture, Isaiah 40:31, which states: "Those who wait on the Lord shall renew their strength; they shall mount up with wings like eagles, they shall run and not be weary, they shall walk and not faint."

The idea kept creeping into my mind. Wait on the Lord. Then I received what I consider now to have been a mini-miracle. It was 10:00 p.m. at night when Vonette Bright, co-founder of Campus Crusade for Christ and leader of the ministry "Women Today" rang my phone. She said she had been meaning to call me for weeks, and felt particularly moved to do so that night. She told me that she needed to tell me how strongly she believed that God had a place for me. She didn't know what that place was any more than I did. But she told me to wait. Wait on the Lord. She reminded me that God had not placed me up on a shelf. He had not forgotten me. I just had to keep waiting.

I'm not going to say that the next morning I woke up to find my life tied up with a neat little bow. I still was clueless as to what God wanted me to do. But I started to take proactive steps toward the ministry that I knew in my heart was what He wanted for me. I waited. I got a part time job that was just that . . . a job, not a career, so I wouldn't be distracted. I waited. I talked with godly men and women in order to receive counsel and network. And I waited.

Months later, things began to fall into place. I was accepted on staff with Campus Crusade for Christ and was allowed to pursue a speaking ministry to college women. My schedule began to fill, and a fledgling ministry was born.

Today I still have to fight off worry, because this ministry does not come with guarantees. But I love it. I'm doing what I know God wants me to do, at least for now. He's welcome to step in anytime and change my direction if He so desires. I realize now that waiting is part of the Christian life. We must wait on God and by faith take the action we believe He wants us to take at the time. It is not a perfect science, but it sure beats worrying.

If you are struggling today with worry and you find

your heart is anxious, I encourage you to decide right now if you are a Sarah or a Hannah. Both were women of faith, but one got there a bit faster than the other. Make a conscious decision to wait on the Lord to carry out His perfect will for your life. Remember that He uses times of trial to not only increase our faith but to mold us into the beautiful women of character He knows we can be.

As mentioned earlier, listening to music helped me in my "waiting process." The words to one of the songs encouraged me to wait on the Lord instead of worrying. It's called "In His Time."

In His time, In His time
He makes all things beautiful in His time.
Lord please show me every day
As You're teaching me Your ways
That You do just what You say
In Your time.[1]

This song is so simple and to the point, but so very true. He does make all things beautiful in His time. Especially things He loves . . . like you and me.

1. In His Time, Maranatha Music.

Chapter 9

Day-to-Day Living
Lopsided or Balanced

Before the network canceled it, I used to really enjoy watching the TV show *Party of Five*. It was a show about five orphaned kids, ranging from two to twenty-five years old. We watched them deal with every tragedy in the book: their parent's death, teen pregnancy, depression, alcoholism, early marriage, early divorce, cancer, domestic violence . . . and the list goes on and on. Interestingly, one of the main characters actually admitted in an episode that his identity came from crises. In a soul-searching moment, the middle brother named Bailey says that he lives from crisis to crisis, waiting for the next thing to go wrong, because that's what he's good at. He's been through so much tragedy that all he knows how to do is fix a problem and wait for the next one to crop up.

Needless to say, that is no way to live. The other day while driving in my car, I was thinking about all the heavy issues we have dealt with in this book, such as feelings of self-worth, compulsions to please others and to be perfect, and dealing with life's worries and tragedies. It struck me that while there are times in our lives that these major things will govern our thoughts, life is not always a chain of dramatic events linked together. In fact, once a lot of these issues are thought through and dealt with, the rest of life is—for the most part—just life. Our lives cannot be lived out the way Bailey, on *Party of Five,* lives—from crisis to crisis. Sure, tragedy is going to take place and bad feelings are going to surface, but we must deal with them and move on.

I believe that if we look at life through God's eyes, we will have the resources we need to do just that. Problems are inevitable, but there's more to life than problems. So in this chapter, we will look at how we should handle day-to-day living, what our goals should be, and what we should be striving for. We'll also ask ourselves how God fits into normal life—you know, when the toilet overflows or bills need paying or company comes over? Just day-in and day-out normal living.

I believe that the Scriptures teach a four-fold formula for leading a balanced life. The Bible outlines it for us in one verse in Luke, describing Jesus: "And Jesus grew in wisdom and stature, and in favor with God and men" (Luke 2:52). The four areas in which Jesus grew are the four areas we must grow in as we live our day to day lives. They are wisdom ("mental"), stature ("physical"), favor with God ("spiritual"), and favor with men ("social"). If we can get these four areas to work together in harmony, then we will be well on our way to living a valuable and productive life, regardless of our circumstances.

To help us understand these qualities in a little more depth, as well as in relation to our femininity, let's look at one more role model. Maybe I've saved the best for last, because of all of the women in the Bible, the most highly praised and well-known is the one simply called the "Proverbs 31 Woman." In case you are unfamiliar with her, read Proverbs 31:10-31. You'll see why everyone agrees that she is the ideal lady.

31:10 Who can find a wife of noble character? For her value is far more than rubies.

31:11 The heart of her husband has confidence in her, and he has no lack of gain.

31:12 She brings him good and not evil all the days of her life.

31:13 She obtains wool and flax, and she is pleased to work with her hands.

31:14 She is like the merchant ships; she brings her food from afar.

31:15 She also gets up while it is still night, and provides food for her household and a portion to her female servants.

31:16 She considers a field and buys it; from her own income she plants a vineyard.

31:17 She begins her work vigorously; and she strengthens her arms.

31:18 She knows that her merchandise is good; and her lamp does not go out in the night.

31:19 Her hands take hold of the distaff, and her hands grasp the spindle.

31:20 She extends her hand to the poor, and reaches out her hand to the needy.

31:21 She is not afraid of the snow for her household, for all of her household are clothed with scarlet.

31:22 She makes for herself coverlets; her clothing is fine linen and purple.

31:23 Her husband is well-known in the city gate when he sits with the elders of the land.

31:24 She makes linen garments and sells them, and supplies the merchants with sashes.

31:25 She is clothed with strength and honor, and she can laugh at the time to come.

31:26 She opens her mouth with wisdom, and loving instruction is on her tongue.

31:27 She watches over the ways of her household, and does not eat the bread of idleness.

31:28 Her children rise up and call her blessed, her husband also praises her:

31:29 "Many daughters have done valiantly, but you surpass them all."

31:30 Charm is deceitful and beauty is fleeting, but a woman who fears the Lord will be praised.

31:31 Give her credit for what she has accomplished, and let her works praise her in the city gates. (NET)

Pretty impressive. Volumes of books have been

written on her virtues, so our goal here is not to pick them all apart. Instead, this chapter provides an overview of what it means to be physically, socially, mentally, and spiritually balanced.

It's often been noted that in the twenty-two verses devoted to this woman, only one verse really deals with her physical appearance. Verse 22 discusses her clothing being finely made and of great quality. That's it! Therefore, we know that in our day-to-day lives, beauty should not receive our primary attention. Yes, we should look our best and be healthy in order to honor the bodies God gave us. We must ensure that we are good representatives on the outside of what a Christian woman looks like on the inside. After all, this world tends to look first and examine later. But this is the least important of the four categories. God is far more concerned with beauty of the heart.

The second category is social. Now what does that mean? Am I talking about how many parties you go to a month? Of course not. When I say social, I'm referring to how we relate to those around us. We know that in relationship to her family, the woman of Proverbs 31 was trustworthy and behaved with integrity in order to bring honor to her husband (verse 11-12). She was also a good mother, for her grown children praised her (verse 28). In addition, she looked after those with whom she worked, making sure that everyone had what they needed (verses 15, 21). Finally she gave to the poor, was involved in charity, and made sure to give to others less fortunate than herself (verse 20).

Right about now you might be saying, "Hold it! Where does this woman find the time to do all these things?" And you're right. I doubt the Proverbs 31 woman is a literal description of what we must do every single day. However, she does show us where our priorities must be. After all, you don't find a verse saying, "She watches television for hours, lounges by the pool all day, and never attempts to leave her comfort zone." Don't get me wrong, relaxation and self-preservation are valid parts of a balanced life, but if we notice that our lives have no time for giving back the good we have received, then something is wrong. A virtuous woman gives what she can, while at the same time keeping herself physically, mentally, and spiritually healthy.

It's fun for me to examine the mental aspect of the Proverbs 31 woman. A lot of people think the Bible has no room for a woman with brains or a woman who excels in the work place. That's not the case here. Go back and read verses 15-19. Whether it's in her house or in the business world, this woman is motivated. She is a diligent worker, a careful planner, and has good sense and perception. She doesn't sit back and let good fortune come to her. She is industrious and uses the gifts God has given her.

For all you ladies who want to shine in the work place, go for it. And for you wonderful women who are committed to raising a family, go for it. Remember, this woman is a symbol, a picture of what virtue is. We know that both choices are prized because at some point in her life, the Proverbs 31 woman has done each. I think what we're looking at here is a woman who gives her all. That is how we must approach each aspect of life that involves the mental or intellectual—and that can be anything from helping kids with their homework to paying the bills, or from getting a good education to building a solid career. I think verse 13 sums it up best when it says "She is pleased to work with her hands." She does what needs to be done with pleasure. Life is not a burden to her. Because her mental attitude is right, even work is a joy.

Finally, we reach the most important of the four categories—the spiritual. The Proverbs 31 woman's character is revealed throughout this chapter. At the beginning we see that her noble character is something far more precious than jewels (verse 10). Furthermore, she has great moral worth and is loving and wise (verse 26). In verse 30, we are told: "Charm is deceitful and beauty if fleeting, but a woman who fears the Lord will be praised." Clearly, the Proverbs 31 woman is summed up by these words. For while we know she is outwardly beautiful, she is more concerned with her relationship with God. That is the mark of a woman with her priorities in check.

The harmonious, balanced life is one where the physical, social, and mental aspects of our character are all outgrowths of the spiritual. In order to keep the spiritual dimension of your life in peak condition, let me recommend four things that should become habits. The first is prayer—intimate conversation with God. Sometimes I like to write my prayers in a journal. Of course, *how* you pray is not as important as the fact that you *are* praying!

Second, read the Word of God daily. Some people like to get a Bible that is designed to be read through in a year. Others enjoy topical studies or Bible studies to get them into the Word. Find your preference or mix it up a little. The crucial thing is that you are saturating your mind with God's love letter to you, daily.

Third, be involved in your local church. I'm not just talking about attending church on Sunday. Make friends with other believers by attending Bible studies or a small group meeting. You need the encouragement of others to grow in your spiritual walk. You also need physical extensions of God's love, and that is found within the family of Christ.

Finally, pray specifically for the Holy Spirit to give you the power and grace to live life as God intended you to live. Ask for strength to meet the day-to-day challenges of life. Don't try to do it in your own power. Whether you are facing something simple or encountering a trying ordeal, the Holy Spirit will enable you to apply what you've learned and put it into practice.

One last thing needs to be reiterated. The Proverbs 31 woman may seem more like Super Woman than an attainable reality, but don't feel intimidated. She is a symbol of what, throughout our lives, we should aspire to be. Acquiring the balance of the Proverbs 31 woman is not a race; it is a marathon that will only be accomplished with steady endurance. Furthermore there is no question that when times of crisis occur, our lives will not be in perfect balance. Nevertheless, if the spiritual dimension of our lives is our center point, then our chance of restoring harmony to day-in and day-out living grows exponentially.

Not too long ago I was in Amsterdam, Holland at a conference for evangelists sponsored by Billy Graham. Because of his health, Dr. Graham was unable to attend. Instead we received a video greeting from him. By his side in the video was his wife Ruth, about whom I had periodically heard, but with whom I was not overly familiar. Yet as I watched her in those brief moments, something about her presence, the twinkle in her eye, and the few words she spoke to us made me want to know more about this wife of the greatest preacher of the 20th century. Upon returning to the states, I found Ruth's biography. The more I have researched the life of this woman, the more I see that a Proverbs 31 woman can exist in modern society.

Ruth's life was never easy. She lived in China as the daughter of missionaries, raised five children partially on her own as her husband traveled so much of the time, and now suffers from a chronic lower back condition. Nevertheless, Ruth Bell Graham has made sure that the physical, social, mental, and most importantly, the spiritual aspects of living are all given their due. In fact, a glance at her 80 years of life indicate that the physical, social, and mental aspects of life are constant, with one merging into the other so you can't tell where one ends and the next begins. But one thing is certain. The spiritual stays central.

As a college student, Ruth met Billy Graham. He claims to have fallen in love at first sight, writing a note to his mother saying that he loved Ruth and would marry her because she looked like his mother. (Billy's mom later confessed to burning the letter for fear of offending Ruth with Billy's analogy!) But Billy saw more in Ruth than just the physical. He met a woman who was so socially concerned that she wanted to be a missionary in Tibet, even if it meant she never married. Of course, we know Ruth's mission field changed when she married Billy. She became his strength and joy as well as the mother of five children, who she sought to raise with the fine balance of strength and God's compassion. It worked, for each one has gone into the ministry (talk about children rising up and calling a woman blessed). We also see the mental aspect of Ruth emerge, particularly in her writing. She expresses herself through poetry and is the author of six books. Throughout her life she has used her wisdom to minister to those overseas as well as to the downtrodden and drug addicted in her own backyard.

Sounding like Super Woman yet? Well, the clincher is her devotion to God. Rising early to have time with the Lord and praying and reading her Bible before lying down to sleep has been her life-long pattern . . . beginning as a student, carrying into her frenzied days of motherhood, and still going strong as she and Billy face their golden years. I love how one writer describes her incredible life:

> Paul wrote to the Corinthians: "You are our letter, written on our hearts, known and read by everybody (II Corinthians 3:2). Ruth Graham's life, aching back and all, is a letter crafted espe-

cially for people like me . . . . It's got to hurt, bearing the physical repercussions of gutsy living while putting your own well-being on the line . . . . Ruth Graham's 80 years provide a picture of the sweet sacrifice of the martyrdom of a long life. It is a letter that should be known and read by everybody.[1]

There's no question that Ruth is a Proverbs 31 woman. However, you don't have to be the wife of a famous evangelist to fit into this category. You can be anyone. In fact, countless women with names and faces unknown to the masses could have had their stories told in these pages. Just because they are not public personalities doesn't mean they are any less noteworthy.

God has equipped all women to be well-balanced Proverbs 31 women, including you and me. It's now up to us to take the reigns. It's a big job, but life is not really exciting until we have a goal—a supreme goal—like becoming the women God created us to be.

1. Zoba, Wendy. Christianity Today, June 2000: 84.

Chapter 10

A Chasing of the Wind
Emptiness Or Fullness

Though I like to think of myself as a fairly disciplined person, I have to admit that there's one thing that can sidetrack me—a good TV show. One of my favorites is *Ally McBeal*. Sure it's quirky, but it usually has an underlying message that, believe it or not, can be quite profound. Such was the case with an episode I recently saw. Ally, a lawyer, was defending a man who was fired from his job because he claimed to have seen a real live unicorn. The argument offered to the judge on the man's behalf was that it's not so strange for a lonely, depressed person to imagine seeing something considered lucky (like a unicorn) in order to feel like there's hope in a world that tends to lack meaning. So if a guy can conjure up a unicorn to give his life a little purpose, more power to him. The judge agreed, and the man got his job back.

Though the show is a bit odd, it rarely fails to get me thinking. Even in a light-hearted, fictitious TV program, people are looking for meaning and purpose. I think it's something we can't help but want to find. Some people look for it in their work, others in fame, and still others in fortune. Some people look to destructive things like alcohol and drugs to fill the empty void in their lives. For a person like me, achievements and the opinions of others are usually at the top of the list as meaning producers. And then of course, there are the folks who look for unicorns.

The point is simple. We all want meaning, purpose, and worth. So what do we do to get all that? Typically we try to manufacture those things, as though meaning, purpose, and worth were things that could be created if we could just get the right ingredients together. Let me share with you the words to one of my favorite songs, which capsulizes this problem that so many people face. It's called "*A Chasing of the Wind.*"

> Every heart is filled with longing
> To be free from all life's pain
> But the search through earthly pleasures
> Always ends in vain
> Only God who made the Heavens
> Can satisfy our souls
> Apart from Him and all His meaning
> All things fail as they begin
> And hearts deceived can only know
> A chasing of the wind.[1]

The words of the song describe exactly what my predicament was on that horrible, tear filled morning of my junior year in high school, which I shared with you at the beginning of this book. I had gone for months and months feeling such pain in my heart as I used every human solution imaginable to deal with an empty soul. Predictably nothing ever worked. With each new attempt at producing meaning—winning pageants, earning good grades, starving to look perfect—I only wound up feeling worse. That is the essence of "a chasing of the wind."

Perhaps you've tried to find meaning and purpose in life by experimenting with a myriad of different "solutions," and none of them are cutting it. You are not alone in your struggles! Even the wisest man who ever lived shared our frustrations.

Thousands of years ago, King Solomon reigned over God's chosen nation, Israel. Solomon was known far and wide for his great God given wisdom, which God promised would surpass anyone who had or ever will live (I Kings 3:12). Yet in the book of Ecclesiastes, the wise King Solomon tells of his struggle with determining the meaning of life. It was King Solomon who first coined the phrase "A chasing of the wind." In chapter two of Ecclesiastes, Solomon tells us that he looked for life's meaning in pleasure, food, drink, work, money, art, and relationships with women. After trying everything, here's what the wisest man who has ever lived concluded: "As I looked at everything I had tried, it was all so useless, a chasing of the wind, and there was nothing really worthwhile anywhere" (Ecclesiastes 2:11 TLB).

I have certainly felt Solomon's discouragement. After I visited the counselor that unforgettable winter day, it took me a long time to start thinking clearly about myself. Because I was so used to running from one thing to the next in order to produce my own meaning and purpose, stopping long enough to take a good hard look at my current place in life was tough. I didn't like what I saw. In a state of utter despair, I concluded along with Solomon that "there was nothing really worthwhile anywhere."

Needless to say, I craved a new perspective. That's when I remembered something that my fourth grade teacher, Mrs. DeVelder, used to say. Mrs. D.V., as we called her, was a fitness nut and had more energy than anyone I had ever met. Her zeal for life, however, didn't come from exercise. One day she told the class her favorite Bible verse, John 10:10. It records Jesus as saying "I have come that you may have life, and have it to the full." Mrs. D.V. kept repeating the last word "full" over and over again with overflowing energy and excitement. Even as a little fourth grader, I knew she believed Jesus' promise of a full life and that her passion came from living out His words.

As I looked back from my discouraging place in life and remembered Mrs. D.V.'s favorite Bible verse, I realized that I definitely was not following in her footsteps. In fact I knew I was living the opposite of a full life, in spite of doing a million things to make me feel full. In an instant I knew I wanted nothing more than to trade in all the false emptiness in my life for a fullness that can only come with knowing the truth. A powerful transformation came when I discovered a relationship with the only person who offered the amazing promise of a full life—the person of Jesus Christ.

If you have been relying upon external factors to generate meaning and purpose, then you know exactly why I needed to look to Jesus's promise. Clearly I had spent too much time with counterfeit solutions. Our only hope is to put our faulty lens aside and pick up the one God offers us. Because He made us with a desire to feel worthwhile, He is the only One who can give our lives true meaning. The great philosopher Blaise Pascal put it this way: "There is a God-shaped vacuum in the heart of every person that cannot be filled by any created thing, but only by God our Creator." When we see God as our only hope and source of fulfillment, there's no question as to what we must do. We must let our souls be satisfied by Him and Him alone.

Living a full and purposeful life is what God intended for His children all along. Life was never meant to be void of meaning. In the Garden of Eden, man and woman had incredible fellowship with God and were blessed by Him (Genesis 1:28). Unfortunately, they chose to go their own separate ways from God, and this fellowship was broken.

This is what the Bible means when it speaks of sin. It is going our own way, away from God. It is saying by word or action "God, You go Your way, I'll go mine. I don't need You, God, I can run my own life." This is what mankind chose to do, and the results were disastrous. Today we see the results of sin in such horrible things as murder, abuse, and racism. It is also seen in offenses such as lying, cheating, and greed. It is also a dark presence that seeps in and robs us of our peace and joy. Sin is the source of hurt, pain, and alienation. It causes us to depend on our humanity to find worth. If we stop relying on God, ignore Him, and choose to trust in ourselves, we break fellowship with Him. From that moment we cheat ourselves out of experiencing the fullness that God wants to bring to each one of our lives.

I'll never forget the story I heard about a man who walked into the office of a psychiatrist and said to the doctor, "I have lost my ability to laugh. If you can't do something to make me happy, when I leave your office, I will commit suicide." The psychiatrist talked for hours with this man, but couldn't get anywhere with him. Suddenly, the doctor had an idea. He remembered that the weekend before he had taken his little boy to the other side of the city to see a circus. In that circus was the funniest clown they had ever seen. They laughed through the entire show and all the way home. That clown was the hit of the circus. The psychiatrist thought that if he could somehow get the depressed man sitting in his office to see that clown, surely the clown could do something to cheer the man. The doctor invited the man to go with him to see the clown. The man looked down at the floor and was silent. Finally he shook his head and said, "I'm sorry, but I cannot go with you. For you see . . . I am that clown." A few days later, that funny circus clown committed suicide.

Nearly every day when we turn on the news or pick up the paper, we see the sad stories of people who, feeling as hopeless as the clown, decide to end their lives. These people are often famous, wealthy, and seem to have everything in the world going for them. Tragically, like the clown, they are laughing on the outside but crying on the inside. The reason? Their fellowship with God has been broken by the ever-present problem of sin. Sin is not just acts of evil. Sometimes sin is no more than willful independence, with us believing that we can run our lives better than the Creator. It is this attitude that separates us from God and keeps us from experiencing true meaning and purpose in life.

God's word gives the solution to this problem. The Bible is clear that the only hope for the problem of sin is God's provision of His Son, Jesus Christ. Now, sometimes you'll hear people say, "I believe there are many ways to God. This Christian belief is too narrow." Well, the problem with that statement is that God says there is only one way to God. John 14:6 records Jesus as saying, "I am the way, the truth, and the life. No man comes to the Father except through Me." Doing good works, going to church, participating in religious or philosophical rituals may contain some measure of goodness in themselves, but they are powerless to do anything about the problem of our separation from God. It is Jesus alone who bridges the gap between God and mankind.

The Bible says that all have sinned and have fallen short of God's ideal for their lives (Romans 3:23). It then goes on to say that the penalty for our sin is death—not just physical death, but a spiritual death that will keep us eternally separated from our Creator (Romans 6:23). God takes our sinning against His holy and righteous character very seriously. However, He also takes things like grace, mercy, and love equally as seriously. The following story illustrates God's justice and His desire to give loving grace.

There once were two best friends who attended law school together. After they graduated, one became a very prominent attorney and later a judge. The other man became involved in several illegal activities and later was arrested. Eventually he was brought to trial before his one-time friend, the judge. Naturally everyone wondered what the judge would do with his friend. Thinking the judge would try to go easy on his old friend, the courtroom was surprised when this judge passed the heaviest fine the law would allow. But what really shocked the crowd was what the judge did next. He stepped down from the bench, removed his robe, took out his checkbook, paid the fine himself, and allowed his friend to go free.

This illustrates what God has done for each one of us. God's love would have gladly forgiven us when we sinned against Him, but His holiness, righteousness, and justice could not allow it. Like the judge, He passed upon humanity the heaviest penalty possible. But then in His love, the God who created the universe stepped out of eternity and into time, visiting planet earth in the person of Jesus Christ. Because of His great love for us, it was the most natural thing imaginable for Jesus to pay with His life the penalty for our sins. The price that He paid was death on a cross. The crucifixion has been described as the cruelest and most hideous form of death ever to be devised in the history of mankind. Because we could do nothing to reach God, Jesus Christ had to do what we couldn't. That is why 2000 years ago, on a cross of wood, Jesus died in our place for our sin (II Corinthians 5:21). In doing so He removed the barrier of sin and bridged the gap that for so long had separated humankind from God.

God did His part in restoring His relationship with you and me when He sent Jesus. But there is still something we must do if we are ever to experience the fullness that God intended for our lives. With the barrier of sin gone, we must decide if we want to accept God's offer of a relationship with Him. The way a person comes into that relationship is simply by expressing that desire to God in an attitude of prayer.

In the last book of the Bible, Jesus extends the following invitation: "I stand at the door (of your life) and knock. If anyone hears My voice and opens the door, I will come in" (Revelation 3:20). But remember, Jesus is a gentleman. He won't force His way into anyone's life. He will only come when we invite Him to do so.

When I was a confused and questioning 16 year old, I had heard time and time again the facts about Jesus dying for my sins. I had decided years before that I wanted a relationship with God and had asked Him to come into my life. Yet years later I was still not living the full kind of life that God had promised. Looking back, I firmly believe that the problem was all in my perspective. I thought that a relationship with God was merely theoretical. I didn't realize that His presence in my life wasn't just something mystical that would start at eternity. It was there for me every single day if I wanted it. He was ready to give me a daily adventure that offered all of the fullness I would ever need. I just couldn't see it. Then one day I heard something that completely changed the way I looked at my relationship with God.

There was a man whose job was to raise and lower a giant bridge over the Mississippi River, so the ships could go through and the trains could go over the bridge. One day he took his eight year old son with him to work. The bridge was up, a ship had just gone through, and a train was coming. The man started to lower the bridge when he heard a horrible scream behind him. He turned around to see that his little boy had slipped and fallen down among the giant gears of the bridge. He knew that if he raised the bridge back up he could save his son's life; but he also knew the train would be wrecked and hundreds would be killed. He had to make a decision. And as he lowered the bridge, he had to watch and listen to the death of his only son as he was crushed among the giant gears of the bridge. As the train went by, a number of people on the train waved at this man as they went merrily on their way, unaware of the sacrifice this father had made by allowing the death of his own son in order to save their lives.

Likewise, 2000 years ago, God had to watch the death of His only son on the cross when He could have stopped it at any moment. The Bible says that God so loved the world (you and me), that He gave His Son. Yet today so many of us, like the people on the train, go through life merrily on our way, just waving at God as we go through, ignoring the sacrifice He has made for each one of us personally.

God's ways are so different than ours. Hearing this story allowed me a glimpse of His perspective. I learned that sending Jesus was His way of saying, "Here I am. I loved you so much that I gave My Son to restore My relationship with you. It was nothing you did or ever could do. You don't have to perform for Me. I want to give your life meaning and purpose, just because I love you. Please let Me." God offers an outrageous gesture of love that cost Him His most precious treasure. He did it for one reason: to give us life. Not a life of hopelessness, not a life of despair, but a life with the richest meaning imaginable.

Learning this amazing truth did wonders for me. I was almost instantly freed to stop my futile attempts at trying to squeeze meaning and purpose out of life. For the first time I was able to quit the performance games and start accepting God's loving provision for my life. The potential of this relationship had been present in my life for years, from the very moment I had asked Christ to be my Savior. But I had to realize the power that came from a relationship with God in order to experience all of the fullness He intended my life to have. My soul finally found its worth in a real, day-in and day-out relationship with the Living God.

If you have never entered into such a relationship

or if you have never understood what it means to be in this relationship with God, then think carefully about the following.

A genuine relationship with God through Jesus Christ is the only hope you will ever have of being a significant citizen, wife, mother, student, career woman, or person who lives her life with any robust sense of worth. He gives you the opportunity to have a life bursting with meaning and purpose. He gives you the chance to truly satisfy your soul.

Isn't it time for you to stop chasing the wind?

1. McHugh, Phil and Nelson, Greg. "A Chasing of the Wind." Gentle Ben Music, 1991.

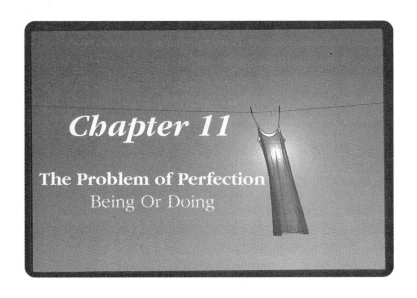

Chapter 11

The Problem of Perfection
Being Or Doing

I have some bad news. It's better that we face it now, instead of being surprised at the last page of this book! I will be perfectly honest—entering into a personal relationship with God through Jesus Christ does not make all of your struggles and problems go away.

Chances are if you were insecure about your looks before becoming a Christian, you will still be so after. If you could have won the award for the World's Number One People Pleaser, guess what? You are probably still in the running. And if you try to be perfect in order to feel good about yourself, perfection is still where you're going to look when you need confidence and reassuring.

"So what's the up side?" you ask. "Becoming a

Christian has to make some difference in my day to day struggles, doesn't it?" Well, you know those problems and struggles you have? Now you have a secret weapon by your side to deal with them. You don't have to fight alone. You have all of the resources that the Creator of this universe saw fit to give you, and you can find each one of them listed in God's Word.

Let's tackle a final problem with which most women struggle to some degree: perfectionism. Perfection is an unattainable goal. Here's a definition I found that nails the entire concept on the head:

> Perfectionism is rooted in the lost recollection of Paradise. Within every believer is an internal barometer of how things ought to be, a deep yearning for the perfection that only heaven will bring. Something inside knows that no matter how good things are—they should be better. One day they will be, but not now. Knowing how it could be while living with how it actually is often causes an unhealthy tension.[1]

Do you know anything about this "unhealthy tension?" I sure do. I see it manifested all around me every day. I feel this tension when my house is cluttered and the laundry is piled high. I feel it when I'm having a bad hair day. I even feel tension when the brand new watch I received for my birthday winds up with a big scratch on it a week later. However these things aren't life and death problems. So why are we talking about perfectionism at all? The reason for this focus on perfectionism is that sometimes it can indeed be extremely life impacting. Let me give you an example.

I was a student until the age of twenty-five, when I graduated with my Master's Degree. During my high school, college, and graduate school years I was a straight A student. Sometimes those grades came easily for me. Other times, it was like pulling teeth to earn an A. Of all my subjects, math was my worst. It didn't matter what area of math, it was all difficult for me. Since I had to see a nice row of perfect A's on my transcript, I spent hours upon hours studying. I would nearly always end up in tears, placing myself under tremendous stress. When I finished my work, I would check where I had placed it several times, just to make sure the paper hadn't moved from my backpack. I even had dreams (and still do, occasionally) of being so far behind in my math class that I would be kept from graduating. I guess you could say I was obsessed. It doesn't take a rocket scientist to see how unhealthy such an obsession was. Was the discipline of mathematics really all that important to me? No. But being perfect was. So I let something as silly as getting an A in a course literally dominate my life.

We all have our own version of math class. Maybe you let the need for a perfect relationship control you. Perhaps you aren't happy until the number on the scale says what you want it to say. You could even be so caught up in perfection that you don't feel you deserve to live unless every category in your life is perfect. I have known such people, which is why I could say earlier that perfectionism can be life and death.

Whether you struggle a little or a lot with the need

to reach an unreachable ideal, something has to be done to fix the problem of perfection. We have to tap into our arsenal of weapons that God has given us to combat the myth that perfection is within our grasp, and that reaching it will make our lives complete, fulfilled and happy. As you know the only way to dispel the darkness of a lie like perfectionism is by shining the light of God's truth directly on the problem.

The first thing about perfectionism which we must address is the myth that self-worth comes through what we do. This faulty perspective turns people into "human doings" and keeps them from existing as God intended them to exist—as human beings. Think about how often the first question out of our mouths when we meet someone is, "So what do you do?" Do you see how prone we are to let the person's response to that question shape our perspective of them? If he says a doctor, we think: "makes lots of money; my parents would approve." Or if she says she's a model, we think: "maybe she's pretty, but I bet she's not too smart." You see we've pigeon-holed these people without knowing anything about who they really are. We just know what they do. It tells us nothing about what really matters— their characters.

Just as we define others by what they do, we are just as guilty when it comes to defining ourselves in the exact same way. That's where perfection comes in. If you are not satisfied with your level of achievement or do not have a list of perfect accomplishments to answer the "what do you do?" question, then you feel miserable. So perfection drives you. Perfection is like a never-ending cloud that hangs over your head to make sure you keep doing great things. Yet all the while you're missing the mark. Sadly, your emphasis is on *what* you want to become, not on *who* you want to become.

You're now in quite a quandary. You know you need to "be," but you're still hung up on the word "do." I think I can help you. My pageant years were a great time of learning. They taught me one valuable lesson in particular: all of my accomplishments would soon pass, but how my character developed was lasting. You can tell which beauty queens have learned the difference between being and doing by listening to their farewell speeches. It never fails. Most of them will say how they wish they could do it all over again. Those are the women who never took the time to participate in self-definition outside of their accomplishment of winning the pageant. Contrast those girls with the ones whose farewell speeches express excitement over pushing forth and seeing what awaits them. These are the women who have let their year as Miss Pageant Girl USA actually develop their characters. They worked to learn their genuine identities—both the strengths and the weaknesses. It is this type of woman who understands the difference between being and doing.

The Scriptures make it very clear that our Heavenly Father is far more interested in who we are in Him than what we do for Him. One example of this is found in Matthew 5:23-24. A man offering sacrifices is instructed to leave it and go to his brother, because he has a relationship that needs to be restored first. There is an aspect of this man's character which demands change before he can continue serving God through sacrificing. It is not a ritualistic, religious action that impresses God; He doesn't care what you do as much as He cares about who you are. The next time you feel compelled to focus on doing something perfectly, but you realize that the end result will only add another line to your resume and not another aspect to you character, I would invite you to say this with me: "To become the one I was created to be . . . Isn't that my great work in life?" *"To become the one I was created to be . . . Isn't that my great work in life?"* (I. Trobisch, The Confident Woman, 9). That is one of my all time favorite quotes. It makes becoming—not doing—our most important work. The reason this saying has become the theme of my life is that it reminds me that only one "work" in my life is truly important: the work of becoming the one I was created to be by my Heavenly Father.

Now that we have a new way of responding to perfectionistic urges, we need a role model. Unfortunately the term "role model" is very pageanty. In fact, "Who is your role model?" is one of the most common questions asked of competitors. I now ask this question as a judge. It's fun to hear the answers. The girls tell me in their interviews that their role models are rock stars, actresses, sports heroes, or the ever popular Oprah Winfrey. The number one answer in every pageant is that the best role model is "my mom." A good mom always has some noble quality of personhood. She has a character worthy of admiration. Thus, the best role models are not always those who have excelled in a particular field or profession; they more often are those who excel in the field of life.

Just as pageant contestants have role models, we need Biblical role models for dealing with life's challenges. That's why I've presented you with numerous biblical personalities to look to as examples. When it comes to dealing with perfectionism, I believe we have an excellent choice offered to us in Scripture. In fact, she was one of Jesus' closest friends. Her name was Mary, the sister of Lazarus and Martha.

> As Jesus and his disciples were on their way, He came to a village where a woman named Martha opened her home to Him. She had a sister called Mary, who sat at the Lord's feet listening to what He said. But Martha was distracted by all the preparations that had to be made. She came to Him and asked, "Lord, don't you care that my sister has left me to do the work by myself? Tell her to help me!"

> "Martha, Martha," the Lord answered, "you are worried and upset about many things, but only one thing is needed. Mary has chosen what is better, and it will not be taken away from her." (Luke 10:38-42, NIV)

From the way this story begins, one thinks that Martha is going to be the hero. Suddenly Jesus is reprimanding her and praising Mary. The first time I read this passage, I was shocked by what Jesus said. I thought that He would admire Martha's hard work and tell Mary to help her. That's not what He did at all.

Jesus actually was displeased that Martha would let her work distract her from the responsibility of building her character by listening to His teachings. He seems to prefer the way Mary sat at His feet with a heart focused on Him.

This is not to say that working hard is unimportant, on the contrary, books such as Proverbs tell us that laziness is to be despised and hard work is to be praised. However in the story of Mary and Martha, laziness is not contrasted with hard work. In this case we are seeing the difference between someone who has her priorities straight and someone who does not. Mary knew that she had little time with Jesus and needed to soak up all He had to say. Martha neglected this "one thing" that Mary was committed to—learning the character of Jesus. This is why Mary is our role model. She knew that who she was in the eyes of Jesus was much more important than what she did. Martha may very well have been a perfectionist, but Mary just focused on spending time with Jesus and being the one He created her to be. What an example for us!

If you or I could attain perfection, there would have been absolutely no reason for Christ to have died for our sins. The reality is that we are not perfect. We make mistakes. We sin. We fall short of the ideal every day. We need to take a few lessons from this.

First, we need to give up the notion that any degree of personal perfection can do anything to bring us closer to God. Remember—this is why Christ died: to bring us to God. This should truly free us up from the need to strive after perfection.

Second, God has not taken us this far in our relationship with Him to leave us with no hope of attaining that which is truly important—a character patterned after Jesus. That is why we have the Scriptures, with examples of people, timely counsel, and practical commands, which can help us be all that we can be as Christians (Philippians 1:6; 3:12-14).

Third, we have the Holy Spirit. Every believer receives the power of the Holy Spirit to do what God desires us to do. The gift of the Spirit is given at the exact moment we first invite Jesus into our lives. From that time forth, the Holy Spirit is with us every day. Therefore as Christians, the whole idea is not to try and "get" more of the Holy Spirit. It's just the opposite. We need to let the Spirit "get" more of us. When we give ourselves to Him through humble prayer, asking Him to help us live our daily lives, then He is faithful to teach us and enable us to be what we were created to be (I John 2:27, Galatians 5:22-24).

And there it is! That is the Christian life in a nutshell—being who God wants us to be through the power of the Holy Spirit. You don't have to be perfect. You don't have to be defined by what you do. You don't have to live up to unrealistic expectations. You don't have to conquer the world with Herculean accomplishments. You just have to be who God created you to be—His imperfect, but unconditionally loved child.

This still may mean we wrestle with issues for a time, wanting to tear our hair out as we confront those things that are painful and daunting. Yet like our role models that have gone before us, we know the job is doable. We have seen ourselves through God's eyes, and once our eyesight has been adjusted, there's no going back. We wouldn't want to. We've seen what life can look like with a brand new perspective, and it's looking pretty good.

1. NKJV Woman's Bible Commentary, 1970

Chapter One
Study Questions

Who do you most commonly look to when you want to find self-worth and acceptance?

Why do you think women tend to compare themselves with others?

In what particular areas do you think your perspective of yourself is different from God's perspective? What do you expect would happen if you adopted His perspective in place of your own?

Chapter Two
Study Questions

How prone are you to listening to what society says about beauty? On a scale of one to ten, how much does it bother you if you can't look like the billboard image?

Of the six traits we examined of an inwardly beautiful woman, which are your strongest? Which traits need improvement?

Read Proverbs 31:13-31. Write as many characteristics as you can find that describe a beautiful woman in God's eyes. Commit to developing one of those traits (or one we discussed) in your life.

Chapter Three
Study Questions

Are you going through an event which has you thinking that God isn't fair? Think about how you feel. How are you responding?

What actions could you be taking to be proactive instead of bitter?

Read Proverbs 16:1-9 which discuss God's sovereignty. How does that passage encourage you to trust that God's will ultimately prevails in all circumstances?

Chapter Four
Study Questions

What person are you most tempted to try to please? Why do you think that is?

What steps can you take to ensure that you ask yourself the filtering question "Will doing what this person wants from me help or hinder my becoming the person God wants me to be?"

Read Acts 5:26-32, Galatians 1:10, and I Thessalonians 2:4. How do these Scriptures encourage you to obey God instead of people?

Chapter Five
Study Questions

How good are you at accepting the free gift of God's love? If it's difficult for you, why?

Identify your own scarlet letter. What do you carry around that makes you feel unworthy of God's love?

Read Psalms 8 and 139. How special and unique do these Scriptures say you are to God? Keep returning to these verses whenever you are tempted to believe you are unloved by God.

Chapter Six
Study Questions

Do you struggle with self-esteem? If so, what things contribute to your negative self-perspective?

Describe in your own words the difference between self-esteem and Christ-esteem. How are they the same and how are they different?

Memorize the two verses that help build Christ-esteem (II Corinthians 10:17 and Ephesians 1:6). How do these verses encourage you to remember your personal worth?

Chapter Seven
Study Questions

Think back over your past relationships, and maybe even the one you're in now. Have you looked to those relationships for self-worth and to make you feel complete?

Develop a list of non-negotiable character qualities for your future mate. Are these traits that you already possess or do you need to work on developing some of them?

Read the Song of Solomon, and if you're really committed, read a wonderful book on the characters of Solomon and the Shulamite: The Book of Romance by Tommy Nelson.

Chapter Eight
Study Questions

About what do you worry most? What is causing you to worry right now?

Read Matthew 6:25-34. What does the Lord say about how much He cares for you and your needs? How does this encourage you not to worry?

Memorize Isaiah 40:31. How will remembering this verse teach you to wait on the Lord instead of worrying?

Chapter Nine
Study Questions

Which area do you need to focus on bringing into balance with the others—the physical, social, mental, or spiritual?

What practical things could you do to get your life in balance? (Read the suggestions in the chapter if you need some ideas.)

Find a woman in your own life who is a practicing Proverbs 31 woman—your mother, grandmother, neighbor, teacher. Use her as your role model for day-to-day living.

Chapter Ten
Study Questions

To what do you look to in life to give you meaning and purpose? How satisfying has that proven to be?

Read Ecclesiastes 2:1-17, pay special attention to what King Solomon used to try to find fulfillment in his life. Do you agree with his conclusions?

Read and think about Jesus' promise of a full life in John 10:10. Are you currently experiencing this abundant living?

If you have never made the decision to enter into a relationship with God, you may wish to consider the following prayer. This prayer is very similar to the one I prayed when Jesus came into my life. It is not the words that are important . . . it is the attitude of your heart. God knows if you are sincere. If you are, here is the prayer:

Lord Jesus, I need you. I admit that I have sinned by going my own way from you. Right now I ask you to come into my life, forgive my sins, and make my life meaningful, purposeful, and what you want it to be. Amen.

Chapter Eleven
Study Questions

With what areas of perfectionism do you struggle? (Work, looks, relationships or something else?)

What changes can you make in your life to be more like our role model Mary and less like Martha?

What does the phrase "To become the one I am created to be—isn't that my great work in life" mean to you?